HEBREWS
The Fulfillment of Faith

Let us fix our eyes on Jesus, the author and perfector of our faith, who for the joy set before Him endured the cross, scorning its shame, and sat down at the right hand of the throne of God.

Hebrews 12:2

Written by Howard Kramin

Edited by Debb Andrus

CONCORDIA PUBLISHING HOUSE • SAINT LOUIS

Series editors: Thomas J. Doyle and Rodney L. Rathmann

Manufactured in the United States of America

11   12   13   14   20   19   18   17

Contents

Introduction

Welcome to a study of one of the most profound books of the New Testament. If you are looking for a model to follow, a cause with which to identify, you'll find it here. If you are looking for some serious study, for solid food instead of baby food, you'll enjoy this study. This first-century letter to the Hebrew Christians is heavy on theology and is filled with all kinds of practical applications for Christian life in this century. But above all, it points us to the Fulfillment of Faith—Jesus Christ—the one who saves us and empowers us to live the new life!

Many Jewish Christians of the first century had been made homeless because of their faith. They lived as pilgrims and strangers in a world that was often hostile to them. They were mocked, tormented, persecuted, and imprisoned. Seeking refuge, many lived in caves. Christians just didn't fit into the Roman style of life. As aliens, they needed encouragement to live for Christ in spite of their circumstances, so the writer of this letter urged them to endure. The necessary courage would come through Jesus Christ, who is first and last and remains forever. Through Jesus, we, too, are made capable of enduring and overcoming all the struggles of life.

God moved the author of Hebrews to use a rich style and language as he penned this treatise. He quoted the Old Testament 29 times and alluded to it more than 50 times as he revealed to us the one person who fulfilled every prophecy—Jesus Christ. Only God knows who wrote this letter. Possibly, desiring to remain anonymous for fear of persecution, the writer intentionally veiled his identity. Scholars have suggested Paul, Apollos, Luke, Barnabas, Priscilla, and Clement of Rome as possible authors. Whoever it was, the author saw the need to build up the Christians under persecution and to encourage them to live to the glory of Jesus.

You will find a challenging message in this book. As you study it, you can be sure that God will build up your faith.

The Leaders Notes in the back of this guide provide direction for each lesson; insights into many Jewish concepts, ideas, and idioms; helps for leading the study; and suggested answers to the questions in this guide.

God bless you richly as you study this book and grow in your faith-life until its fulfillment through Jesus Christ!

Lesson 1

Focus on the Son
(Hebrews 1)

Theme Verse

"In these last days [God] has spoken to us by His Son ... through whom He made the universe" **(Hebrews 1:2).**

Goal

Through study of the first chapter of Hebrews, we pray that the Holy Spirit may help us identify Jesus as God, the only Son, the one who was promised and who appeared on earth to show us the Father; recognize that when we see Jesus, we see the Father; and find special help and comfort in seeing Jesus as the Lord of our life.

What's Going On Here

Christ is superior in every way! All 13 chapters of this letter speak to this one issue. Throughout the centuries, God used the prophets to speak whenever He had a message to deliver. People looked upon the prophets with awe—and often with fear. Sometimes, as God made their voice boxes divine means of communicating truth, the prophets became downright unpopular. Yet, Peter tells us **(2 Peter 1:21),** these men spoke by the Holy Spirit. He empowered them to speak the truth without error. The Word they spoke touched the hearts of people. It still does.

At the close of the New Testament era the message of God to His people was complete. God had spoken a last time. Christ is the end of the message, the exclamation mark. He is God's last Word to the world. Maybe people had revered the prophets; now they were to focus on the Son of God and listen as they had never listened before! In Christ God gave us His ultimate message. Words of salvation come from our majestic Lord, who has supremacy over all things in heaven and on earth (**Colossians 1:15–20**).

In this first chapter, God does not speak primarily of prophets or of angels, but of Jesus. As important and as powerful as prophets and angels are, the Son of God is superior to all of them. Therefore He is the help, the aid, the comfort God has provided for everyone. He can help anyone, even those who think they are beyond help. So don't run from Him! Don't defect! Focus on the Son of God, Jesus Christ, who is superior to every being in this universe! You can count on Him! Cling to Him by the faith He has given you!

Searching the Scriptures

1. **Verses 2–3** give a fascinating introduction to God's Son. Glean from these verses the seven statements that speak so magnificently of Jesus.

a. *spoken to us by his Son*

b. *heir of all things*

c. *radiance of the glory of God*

d. *exact imprint of his nature*

e. *upholds the universe by the word of his power*

f. *made purification for sins*

g. *sat down at the right hand of the Majesty on High*

Notice that all of those statements speak also of God the Father.

2. Knowing Christ is knowing God precisely as He is. What did Jesus say about Himself and the Father in **John 10:30, 38?**

I and the Father are one. The Father is in me and I am in the Father.

3. In **John 14:9** Jesus assured the disciples that when they have seen Him, they have "seen the Father." Read the passage. How do you "see" God the Father in Jesus?

Whoever has seen me has seen the Father.

4. An intimate relationship exists between the Father and the Son. The writer quotes the Old Testament twice **(Hebrews 1:5, 13)** to show that relationship. Which words show that Jesus is superior to the angels and is God?

begotten

sit at my right hand.

5. People generally worship superior, not inferior, beings. Read **verse 6** and then read **Revelation 5:11–13** and **22:8–9.** What instruction is given in each instance?

worship of the Lamb who was slain

John told not to worship angels

6. This chapter contains some of the greatest testimonies that Jesus is God. How does the writer show the "God-ness" of Jesus in

verse 8? *throne, scepter*

verse 9? *anointed*

verse 10? *laid foundation of earth, heavens the work of Jesus' hands*

verses 11–12? *eternally alive*

verses 13–14? *Jesus at right hand angels ministering spirits*

7. First-century Christians knew much about God's angels. They called them "winds" and "flames of fire," referring to their swiftness and to their sweeping effect, which is beyond the control of people. Angels are also "ministering spirits" to render service to humans. Yet, no matter how powerful, how sweeping, or how swift the angels are, not one of them is as significant as the Son of God, Jesus Christ.

In order to increase your knowledge of the angels, jot down what you learn about these created beings of God as you look at the following references:

Numbers 22:21–35 *threatened Balaam*

Psalm 91:11–12 *guarding*

Matthew 13:39, 49 *at close of age will separate evil from righteous*

Luke 1:13, 26–27 *messengers to bring good news*

1 Corinthians 10:10 *destroyed by Destroyer*

Hebrews 1:7, 14 *winds, flames - ministering spirits*

Hebrews 13:2 *strangers may be angels*

1 Peter 1:12 *angels long to look*

8. According to **Hebrews 1:14,** what work do angels do?

ministering spirits sent out to serve

9. Name some of the ways angels serve God's people.

bringing messages guarding

10. What are some words from **Hebrews 1** that emphasize that the Son rules and the angels serve?

"Let all God's angels worship him."

11. What, then, is the relation between the Son and the angels?

The Son rules the angels.

12. In **verses 10–12,** some of the qualities of God are named and applied to Jesus to tell us He is God. List those qualities.

laid foundation of earth heavens work of your hands imperishable eternal life

9

13. Now, in a few words, describe Jesus as you have seen Him in this chapter.

Jesus is God's son.

The Word for Us

1. How does God reveal divine truth?

prophesy
words of Jesus

2. How can you reply to people who claim that God is "speaking" to them?

depends on what they mean by "speaking"

3. What assurance do you get from **verses 11–12** that God is and will remain in control of all things for you through His Son?

His Son is eternally in control of all that is.

4. The character of Jesus, according to **verse 12,** is changeless. What comfort does that give to you when you are in the following circumstances?

• You are awakened at night by a terrible storm.

• You are seeking truth.

• You are suffering an illness.

• You encounter members of cults.

• You hear about terrorism and threats of war.

• You think of your own death.

• You face unemployment.

- You suffer disability.

- You are enduring an economic crisis.

- You anticipate a geographical move that will separate you from loved ones.

Keep a log of how the changeless Christ has helped you in your changing world. Share this at the next meeting of your study group.

5. As you have faced other difficulties in life, to whom have you most often turned?

prayer to the Lord

6. To whom does this lesson urge you to turn?

Jesus is the Lord of life.

7. What assurance has helped you to know that in every moment of life you can focus and depend on Jesus? Memorize **Hebrews 1:1–4.**

heir of all things
exact imprint of Majesty on high

8. Martin Luther's morning and evening prayers conclude with these words: "Let Your holy angel be with me, that the evil foe may have no power over me." Name some other things angels can do for you, a believer in Jesus.

guard us

9. Name some things angels cannot do for you. You may want to begin by looking at **John 3:16.** (Think of those things that are possible only for God.)

Come, Lord Jesus!
Receiving His body and blood
and His forgiveness.

10. Think of some ways in which you will worship Jesus as you sharpen your focus on Him. Take a moment to jot down some words that describe Jesus with which you can give Him praise in your private worship. Then speak your praise to Him in prayer as you focus on the Son.

Closing

Pray together, **Dear Jesus, in You God made His "final speech" to the world, a beautiful statement of His gracious and good will. You are God: we worship You. You are superior to all creation: we submit to You. You are changeless: we depend on You to supply our every need in an ever-changing world. You died on the cross for our sins: forgive us. You rose again on Easter morning: give us Your eternal life and peace. You ascended into heaven: dispatch Your holy angels to touch our physical needs. We pray all this in Your name and by the power of the Holy Spirit. Amen.**

Lesson 2

It's All in the Way You Look at It (Hebrews 2)

Theme Verse

"We see Jesus … crowned with glory and honor" **(Hebrews 2:9).**

Goal

To face the suffering and pain of this world by laying hold of the comfort offered by Jesus, our High Priest who atoned for all our sins and continues to make intercession to the Father for us.

What's Going On Here

Horror! Affliction! Suffering! Pain! We often wish those words were not in our vocabulary! Intellectually we may know that God makes us strong and confident through those experiences. However, at times we may also feel weak in faith and even bitter toward God.

The first-century Christians were often subjected to suffering and pain as a result of public displays of their faith. Many resisted the temptations Satan brought to them when they had to decide to either deny the Lord of their life or suffer pain and death in the arena. But others turned away from their Lord in favor of the comforts of their former years.

We today are tempted to do the same when we face suffering and pain. We often wish that our faith in Jesus would keep suffering away. This temptation seems especially strong when we hear stories of miraculous healings of people once they become Christians. Miraculous healings do happen. Our Lord can heal if He so desires. Yet the consequences of sin remain; our Lord has not promised to heal every ill. In fact, He reminds us of the opposite, "In this world you will have trouble" **(John 16:33)**.

How, then, do you handle suffering and pain? How can you? How will you?

Perspective! That one word suggests the secret to enduring suffering. Different perspectives lead one person to grind to a halt while another grinds through life. Our perspective leads us either to see suffering as cruel (and therefore to blame God) or to stop fighting God and get on with living. Perspective will either destroy or enhance our view of life.

The writer to the Hebrews reminds us that Jesus entered into glory through suffering **(Hebrews 2:9)**. This suffering included His death (as this passage reminds us) as well as the physical abuse that led to it. It also included the suffering of His temptation **(2:18)** and the pain of being rejected by His own people. Jesus helps us resist the temptation to view our suffering as cruel punishment from God. Our High Priest empowers us to gain a new perspective on life, a perspective that believes God helps us "in our weakness" **(Romans 8:26)**. And, suffering reminds us that we are merely human and are waiting for the day when we will be transformed and enter into the new heaven and new earth, where there will be no more sorrow or pain **(Revelation 21:1, 4)**.

Searching the Scriptures

1. **Hebrews 2** begins with an exhortation to remain steadfast in the faith. In our mobile and often permissive society, geographic moves can be accompanied by drifting away from an active spiritual life. What words of **verses 1–4** may help us avoid drifting from the Lord?

We must pay much closer attention to what we have heard, lest we drift away from it, ... disobedience received a just retribution.

2. God, through St. Paul, predicted in **2 Timothy 3:1–9** that drifting from the Lord would occur in the last days. Describe the evidence of that drifting today.

People will be lovers of self, lovers of money, proud, arrogant, abusive, disobedient to their parents, ungrateful, unholy ... not loving good, swollen with conceit, lovers of pleasure rather than lovers of God.

14

3. According to **2 Timothy 3:10–17,** how can we avoid spiritual erosion in our lives?

All Scripture is breathed out by God and profitable for teaching, for reproof, for correction, and for training in righteousness ...

4. When we drift away and err, it is difficult to hear the resulting words of admonition. However, those words are necessary for our spiritual good. What is the "just punishment" referred to in **Hebrews 2:1–3?**

"Just retribution" is what disobedience deserves.

5. In addition to eternal consequences, suffering occurs on earth when people violate God's laws. What are some of the results of breaking God's law concerning

love and respect for one another?

hurt feelings

greed?

things become more important than people

chastity?

unhappiness

coveting?

envy

6. In **Hebrews 2:6–8** the writer refers to **Psalm 8** and **Genesis 1:27–30.** While the writer of **Psalm 8** apparently was writing about humans, the words also point to Jesus, the greatest man. What authority was given to man? to Jesus (see **Hebrews 2:9**)?

everything in subjection under his feet

Jesus crowned with glory and honor because of the suffering of death

7. Since sin entered the world, we can no longer exercise perfect authority over all creatures and cannot even exercise such control over ourselves. How does Jesus help the believer to exercise authority in a way

that is pleasing to God?

prayer
scripture reading

8. Why was Christ's death necessary, according to **Hebrews 2:9?**

He tasted death for everyone.

9. Sin came and conquered the human race. Crisis has followed crisis ever since. We have been unable to handle our last great enemy—death. How has the consequence of sin (death) been conquered? (See also **1 Corinthians 15:50–58.**)

God gives us the victory through our Lord Jesus Christ.

10. Think of the ways people try to obtain glory. Contrast that with the way to glory mentioned in **Hebrews 2:9–10.** Read also **Philippians 2:5–11.** What acts brought glory to Christ?

humility

11. What a comfort to know that we are called children of God! What a joy to know that Christ really came and took on our human flesh and blood! What a blessing to know that He conquered our deadliest enemies! How does this knowledge help us to overcome the fear of sin's punishment? the fear of dying?

Jesus prays for us. His Holy Spirit intercedes for us.

12. We fail to live up to the Lord's Law. We do not even live up to our own expectations. Yet we do not face a condemning judge but a merciful High Priest, Jesus, who confronts our sin, deals with it, and forgives it.

What assurance do you find in **Hebrews 2:14–18** for the nagging fear that you may not be forgiven? How can you put that fear to rest?

Jesus makes propitiation for us.

13. Read **Matthew 4:1–11.** What temptations did Jesus endure?

hunger power worshipping Satan

14. Of all the temptations you face, which of them do you think Jesus faced as He lived in human flesh on this earth?

15. Why, according to **Hebrews 2:18,** can Jesus be your best help in temptation? How can you use His victory to help you when tempted?

He suffered when tempted. Pray.

The Word for Us

1. When you are under pressure and/or facing temptations, do you rely on your own instincts or on the truth of God's Word? Why? What advice do you find in **Proverbs 3:1–5?**

Trust in the Lord.

2. Mention some ways to get out of the rut of relying on human opinion and ingenuity rather than the unmistakable guide of God's Word.

Read the Bible.

3. Our sinful human nature leads us to choose the comfortable rather than the painful, and thus may cause us to sin. Suggest some ways to

a. keep your personal integrity;

Don't lie to yourself.

b. strive for sexual purity;

Avoid books, DVD's that are impure.

c. remain faithful to your faithful God;

Prayer, worship.

d. fight the good fight of faith;

Keep trying.

e. overcome temptations in your life;

Think

f. respond to failures in your life;

Try to learn from them.

g. respond to the failures of others; and

forgive

h. keep a positive outlook on suffering.

Ask Jesus to help.

4. Suffering takes various forms. It may be the grief of losing a loved one, the hurt of words that penetrated like stab wounds deep into your life, or even an indescribable pain. The suffering may destroy your sense of humor and ability to think logically. When you suffer, what strength can you draw from Jesus' suffering? from Jesus' promise to help **(Hebrews 2:17–18)**?

He was human and understands.

5. Take time to reflect on another person with whom you may have had a difference. This time, look with the same compassion on that person that Jesus has had on you. Remember the words Jesus spoke while suffering on the cross, "Father, forgive them" **(Luke 23:34).** How can you make these words a part of your action toward that person? When you are able, tell that person of your love and care.

Forgive

6. When bearing the pain of the loss of a loved one, what assurance does **Hebrews 2** give you?

Jesus is our brother and is able to help those who are being tempted.

7. How can you maintain the perspective that you may enter into glory amid suffering? If time permits, write a paraphrase of **Hebrews 2:9–18**. You'll be surprised how much you will learn through writing it.

8. Read **Philippians 3:7–11** and write down those actions you may take to help you be positive when living through pain and suffering.

Share His suffering

9. Have you had a nagging guilt about a sin or a failure in your life? What assurance do you receive in **Hebrews 2:9, 15?**

10. How can your own suffering give you a greater compassion for others?

Closing

Pray together, **Heavenly Father, sometimes it's difficult to keep a positive perspective on life, especially when we encounter suffering and pain. That's when we need to look again to Your Son Jesus, who entered glory through suffering. Help us always to remember that Your ways are often quite different from our ways, and Your thoughts are higher than ours. Thank You for giving us the exhortations and promises of Your Word. Help us to use them to keep us from drifting away from You and Your purposes in our life. Strengthen us when temptations come. Help us to view the whole world from the perspective of Christ. In His name we pray. Amen.**

Lesson 3

Don't Miss Out on the Rest (Hebrews 3:1–4:13)

Theme Verse

"Fix your thoughts on Jesus" **(Hebrews 3:1).**

Goal

That daily, by the power of the Spirit, we may express gratitude for the grace of God and the Christian life; live with an active, vibrant faith; and eagerly look toward the final day and entry into God's eternal kingdom.

What's Going On Here

Stress! The mere mention of the word may tie our stomachs in knots. Life in a fast-paced world can increase our already stressed lives and relationships. As we search for a little relaxation and relief for our hectic lives, we find a number of exercises, mind-soothing techniques, and even stress-relief clinics. We long for some rest!

When you think of rest, what pictures come to mind? A lazy day on the beach? A hike along your favorite trails? A drive to a choice picnic spot? An afternoon of skiing? Settling down to read a great novel? A quiet conversation in front of the fireplace, where the flames lazily lick away at the wood? Whatever you think of, the idea of rest for most people is delightful! None of us is capable of living with constant stress. It will gnaw away at our very existence the way a beaver chomps away at the tree near the water's edge. Unless we get relief, we will topple just as certainly as the tree that has had its strength cut away.

As critical as stress is in our lives, the writer of Hebrews tells us about something much, much more critical. He warns us of the danger of falling into disbelief. This will eventually cause a heart to harden like a rock.

A glance back at the Old Testament will provide the historical setting for this section of Hebrews. The people of Israel took 40 years to accomplish what could have been done in about two weeks. Why did it take them so long? *Unbelief!* They decided to follow their own way instead of God's way. Sin deceived them into thinking they knew better than God. That led to hardening of their hearts.

The writer clearly states the consequences and punishment of sin. While Israel could have been living a healthy life in a land flowing with milk and honey, the people instead lay dead in the wilderness as God administered divine discipline. Clearly the Lord is displeased with every act of disobedience, rebellion, and unbelief. The warning of this lesson comes to us as fresh today as it came almost 2,000 years ago. God realizes that we need the kind of warning that will keep us alert to the things we cannot afford to forget.

During this lesson you will find that God has provided a rest for us. It's something we can have every moment of our life. Let's find out how!

Searching the Scriptures

Hebrews 3 begins with the word *therefore*. The writer is tying the message of the Gospel (the forgiveness of sins brought to us by Christ Jesus) with the message of warning not to trifle with the Word of God.

Several times the writer also uses another word—*faithful*. We read about the faithful builder, Jesus; the faithful servant, Moses; and the faithful believers, those who continue in faith in Jesus.

1. How do we show that we are faithful, according to **Hebrews 3:6?**

hold fast our confidence and our boasting in our hope

2. Read **1 Corinthians 4:1–2.** You have been entrusted with much from the Lord. What does the Lord require of you? (See also **Micah 6:8.**)

to do justice, to love kindness and to walk humbly with your God

3. Also read **1 Peter 1:3–5.** Notice that both this passage and **Hebrews 3:1–6** speak about our heavenly home. What action do we need to take in order to remain faithful and enter that home? Why are we able to take that action?

see answer to ques. 1

The Holy Spirit helps us! Jesus helps us.

4. To better understand **Hebrews 3:7–11,** look at a bit of Israel's Old Testament history. Read the verses and answer the questions below:

Exodus 17:1–7

a. How was the faith of the people tested?

lack of water

b. How did the people test and try God?

questioning and grumbling

c. What was their sin?

lack of trust and faith

d. How were they reminded of this sin?

staff used to produce miracles in Egypt was used

e. What should they have learned?

God was with them. to bring water from rock

Numbers 13:1–14:4

a. How was the faith of the people tested?

Moses sent people to spy out the land.

b. How did the people test and try God?

They discouraged the Israelites from trying to take the land.

c. What was their sin?

Lack of trust and faith

d. How were they reminded of this sin?

e. What should they have learned?

to trust God

5. When **Psalm 95** was used in the synagogue worship, what reminder of Israel's sin could the people find in **verse 8?**

Meribah — Massah

6. What was the result of their unbelief, according to **Hebrews 3:11?**

God said, "They shall not enter my rest."

7. In **Hebrews 3:12** the writer turns from Israel to the readers—you. God's anger at sin was poured out on Jesus on the cross. What warning does God give you, a believer in Jesus?

Don't fall away from the living God!

8. The devil tempts all Christians to doubt the goodness of God. All fall victim to this sin at times. Then the devil tries to change the doubt into unbelief, a condition in which we have completely lost our trust in God. When Satan succeeds here, he moves to the final step, the hardening of the heart and a resistance to anything that is of God. According to **Hebrews 3:13** how can we help one another overcome sin's deceitfulness?

Exhort one another.

9. Where can we get the strength and the words to encourage one another?

Rely on scriptures.

10. What words do this writer **(3:13)** and the psalmist **(Psalm 95:7)** use to emphasize the urgency of this encouragement?

harden hearts by deceitfulness of sin

11. Remembering to whom this is addressed, whose responsibility is it to offer warnings and encouragement to fellow Christians?

brothers [and sisters] in Christ

12. Read **1 Corinthians 12:12–27.** What motivation for encouraging one another do you find there?

We are all members of the Body of Christ.

13. After the testing mentioned in **Exodus 17** and **Numbers 13** the people felt less confidence in God. An earlier testing at the Red Sea had increased their confidence in God **(Exodus 14:31).** How can tests be turned into rests for believers in Christ?

14. We read about a rest in **Hebrews 4:1–11.** The writer mentions that God rested after He finished all His creating and the people of Israel rested after they entered Canaan. The ultimate rest, however, is the eternal life in heaven at the end of all things. The writer was obviously pointing to this rest throughout these verses.

As people who want to enter God's eternal rest, God instructs us to hear and believe His Word. According to **4:2, 6** what message must we believe?

15. God's Word is called a double-edged sword in **4:12–13.** As such it penetrates our very being, calls us to account by revealing what may be hidden to all humans, and judges our every attitude and thought. Read **John 12:48.** What else does it judge?

The word of Jesus on the last day.

16. What can be hidden from God?

Nothing.

17. Think about the power God gives through His Word. Why would a Christian constantly want to read and study that Word? (Your answer may include some thoughts from **Hebrews 4:2, 6,** and **11.**)

18. The sword of the Word of God also has a healing function, much like a physician's scalpel. What is the message of the Gospel that provides healing for our sin and guilt? (See **Isaiah 53:4–6.**)

... with his stripes we are healed

19. Who will receive this final rest God has provided for His people **(Revelation 2:10)?**

Be faithful unto death and Jesus will give us the crown of life.

The Word for Us

1. A young couple decided that the wedding gift they received from the groom's great-grandmother should become a priceless heirloom, so they kept it folded in its original package and stored it in a drawer. On the 25th anniversary of their marriage, the bride decided to set a beautiful table for dinner using that heirloom, a special lace tablecloth. To her dismay, it fell apart as she took it out of its package. During the years of neglect it had rotted, been partly eaten by moths, and become useless and ruined.

In a similar manner, unless we exercise our faith and are in constant contact with God's Word and sacraments, Satan may cause our faith to become dull, static, and stale.

Think about your life for a moment. Silently review your worship, your Bible study, and your conversations with Christians and non-Christians. What will help you to worship with new vigor?

2. Suggest some changes in worship practices in your congregation to make worship more meaningful.

3. Offer similar suggestions for group and individual Bible studies in your church.

4. Sometimes people become complacent and then depend on the forms of Christianity rather than the real substance of the faith. Do a spiritual inventory of your life. How can you keep your own faith vibrant and centered on God's Word?

5. Read James 5:20. Suppose the words or actions of a fellow Christian show that he or she is slipping from the truth of God's Word. Who has the responsibility to bring that person back to a living relationship with Jesus?

6. Tests from God are not meant to harden our hearts but to purify them **(Zechariah 13:9)**. God does not tempt anyone to sin, but He does test His own people. (Note that when God tests you, He does not *cause* "bad" things to happen to you, but He permits them to happen.) How do you think you would (or how did you) respond if God tested you with an illness? the death of a loved one? a financial loss? an accident?

7. Sometimes we get discouraged when troubles come our way. What encouragement and strength can you find in the words of Job **(Job 1:21; 2:10)**, Jesus **(John 16:33)**, and John **(1 John 1:9)?**

8. Why can't you hide anything from God? Why can you turn to His Word for comfort and help?

9. God will keep His promise of giving an eternal rest. What do you need to enter into that rest?

10. Discuss with other participants in your group how all of you may more effectively hear the Word of God and respond in faith. Agree to give a helping hand to a fellow believer this week that will serve to strengthen him or her, especially as this person is undergoing a time of testing.

Closing

Pray together, **Dear God, just as You rested after creation, so You promise eternal rest in heaven for all the faithful. So many millions have missed that rest because they have not heard and believed Your Word. Through Your Holy Spirit, keep our faith strong and living. Help us to hear Your Word with an open heart and mind. Give us the opportunities to encourage our fellow believers, especially when we notice that they fail to hear and believe Your Word or when they slip from a life of love to You. Keep our faith strong to endure the tests of life that will come our way, so that we may finally, by living to the very end in faith, enter into eternal rest with You in heaven. We pray this in the name of Jesus. Amen.**

Lesson 4

Who Needs It, Anyway?
(Hebrews 4:14–5:10)

Theme Verse

"Let us then approach the throne of grace with confidence" **(Hebrews 4:16)**.

Goal

To describe Jesus as our intermediary, the only one who is able to bring our prayers to the Father's throne, while also expressing confidence that as members of the priesthood of all believers, we can pray directly to Jesus, who accepts us and hears our prayers.

What's Going On Here

"I've never been this far forward in the church before," she said, "except when I take Communion. Isn't this the space reserved for pastors and those with some special qualifications?"

The woman speaking was a new Christian. As far as she knew, the chancel area was "holy ground." Afraid that she would be struck by a bolt of lightning if she trespassed in this place, she stood in fear of approaching the altar.

Many churchgoers believe that no one with unholy feet dare trample this "sacred area." It is reserved for the special servant of God, the pastor. Mishap surely awaits any other who may even by accident enter the arena of the divine. After all, didn't the Lord strike Uzzah dead **(2 Samuel 6:6–7)** for the helpful act of steadying the ark of the covenant as it was being transported? If he met the terror of God while he was trying to be helpful, will not any who wander into sacred territory receive a harsh punishment? Some would elevate the pastor to the position of being the only one who can bring prayers, petitions, and intercessions before God, especially if we expect them to be answered.

The Reformation brought to light a whole new outlook for each believer. As God tells us in **1 Peter 2:9,** every child of God has an open access to His throne. Each Christian is a priest, having open, direct access through Christ to the throne of God. We need no other intermediary than Christ, the sole intercessor for all who call upon Him in faith. Christ is our heavenly representative. He understands us. He sympathizes with us. He feels for us. He is for us! He lives permanently in the heavens! He has entered the "holy of holies" before us and has prepared our entrance into it.

Before we get "neck deep" into the study of the great High Priest in the order of Melchizedek (which we will do in lesson 6), let's take a while to savor our exalted position before the throne of God. We need not be afraid. The way is opened by Christ, the Fulfillment of Faith, who lives to grant us rich supply of all that we need. We can pray to Him. We can ask Him. We indeed need Him. So, don't be afraid. Come to Him!

Searching the Scriptures

The Israelites thought it was dangerous to approach God. They remembered Sinai with its clouds and smoke and thunder. They recalled that after Moses had been in God's presence, his face was too bright to look at. On rare occasions God had spoken to special people. Others had to bring a sacrifice when they wished to approach God. They looked for a high priest to take that offering to the altar of God so that it might be acceptable to the Lord of the universe.

1. Who is the high priest to whom the writer refers in **Hebrews 4:14?**

2. Why can Christians now approach the throne of God without the assistance of an earthly mediator?

3. What role does faith play in our approach to God?

4. Recall the following events in the life of Jesus: His birth, His life on earth, His death on Calvary, His resurrection, His ascension to heaven. Jesus is the great High Priest who has "gone through the heavens." Therefore, He is not only true God but also true _____ .

5. **Verse 15** tells us that Jesus is truly human. How does He differ, however, from all other humans?

6. Look up and read the following passages: **Matthew 8:20; Luke 8:23; 19:41; 22:44; John 4:6–7; 11:35; 19:28.** What human characteristics does Jesus share with us? What are some others?

7. What comfort do you find in the humanness of Jesus as you view your own humanity?

8. Jesus was truly human but yet was perfect and without sin. Why is this so important when you remember He offered Himself to forgive our sins? (See also **1 Peter 1:18–19** and **John 1:29.**)

9. Someone had defined *mercy* as "not getting what is deserved" and *grace* as "getting what is not deserved." How do these definitions offer comfort when you think about a sin you have done? when you need strength in temptations?

10. Jesus extends His arms to us to come to Him unafraid and with confidence. He understands us, He forgives us, and He invites us. Read **1 John 4:17–18.** Why need we not be afraid to approach Him?

11. In **Hebrews 5:1–4** we find a list of certain qualifications and duties of the earthly priests who ministered before the Lord's altar. What are five of these qualifications and duties?

a.

b.

c.

d.

e.

12. Now read **verses 5–10.** How did the heavenly High Priest, Jesus Christ, fulfill the requirements to be an eternal High Priest for us?

a.

b.

c.

d.

e.

13. Compare **verse 7** with **Luke 22:39–46**—a prayer to Him who has the power over death. Which words of Jesus show His reverent submission?

14. Jesus had no sin of His own to carry to the cross, the altar of sacrifice. For whose sins, then, did He offer His life?

15. By one act God accomplished eternal salvation for all who believe in Jesus. How is that stated in **Hebrews 5:9?**

16. Sometimes we sin willfully and know we have sinned. Other times we may not even know how we have sinned. We need not go to an earthly priest to confess our sins. To whom do we go?

17. Skim Jesus' parable in **Luke 15:11–24.** What kind of reception will you, a repentant child of God, receive at the throne of God?

The Word for Us

1. Compare the following pictures of God.
a. The great Ruler of the universe who is somewhat distant.
b. An indulgent grandfather-type of God.
c. A God of power and might, yet understanding, caring, and loving.
d. The immortal, invisible God who is judge of the living and the dead and will surely punish all transgressors.

How has this lesson helped to shape the way you view God? Describe God in your own terms.

2. When we pray, we can go directly to God's throne through our great High Priest, Jesus. How did Jesus say that in **John 15:16** and **14:13?**

3. God is not far away. Because of His own Son, Jesus, who became one with us to bring us to God, He is very near. Name some ways you can continue to build that strong bond with your God.

4. We may not feel free to share everything about our lives with even our most intimate friends, but we can come to God through Jesus with every aspect of our lives. Why does God not judge us in the same way as a friend who knows intimate things about us?

5. When you sin, whether by giving in to temptations or because you are weak and feel unable to stop, what assurance does **Hebrews 4:15–16** give?

6. Sometimes, although we know we shouldn't, we do a sin deliberately. Does God forgive those sins also? Read **Luke 24:47.** What must be present along with forgiveness?

7. Sometimes we commit sins without even knowing we have done them. Although there is no excuse we can offer to God, we can confess those sins, possibly with the words of **Psalm 19:12.** Write those words here as a reminder to use them often as words of confession.

8. Grace is an undeserved gift from God. We live only by God's grace. Forgiveness is a gift of grace. Since we can't earn a gift, what is an appropriate response for the forgiveness Jesus gives?

9. How does **Hebrews 4:14–16** help us when we become anxious about approaching the altar of God in church or the throne of God in prayer?

10. Read **1 Peter 2:9.** What does this verse have to say about all Christians? What is our role?

11. The high priest was more than just an intermediary between God and the people. He also ministered to people on God's behalf. Our pastors do the same. Without putting them on a pedestal, how can we best show our respect for them?

12. Since we are the priests who come to God's throne, and since a priest did not come into God's presence empty-handed, what do these verses say are the sacrifices we are now to bring?
   a. **Romans 12:1**

   b. **Philippians 4:18**

   c. **Hebrews 13:15**

   d. **Hebrews 13:16?**

13. Look again at **Hebrews 5:9.** What assurance does this passage give to you when you feel anxious or afraid? when you feel your faith is weak? when a sin makes you feel guilty? when things are going well in your life?

14. This week try out your "priesthood" in some new or different ways. And, as you do, remember that you have a place before the throne. Act confidently.
   —Look with compassion on someone who is suffering or hurting because he or she made a mistake of weakness.
   —Pray for a friend, a loved one, all leaders of nations, and even an enemy.

—Acting as a priest of God, confidently assure a fearful person of God's "open door policy" through Christ.

—Grow in your Christian confidence by memorizing **Hebrews 4:14.** Then apply it to your daily living.

Closing

Pray together, **Dear Father, You sent Your Son to become our Brother in the flesh and so that He could serve as our perfect High Priest in every way. Only Jesus understands our anxieties, stresses, weaknesses, and temptations. Because He did not sin, He served as the perfect sacrifice for us. We pray to You through Jesus, our High Priest, knowing that through Him we also have been made priests before Your throne. We know we can come to You with all our sin—all our guilt—and be assured of forgiveness. We thank You for this great privilege through the name of Jesus. Amen.**

Lesson 5

Getting Out of the Nursery (Hebrews 5:11–6:20)

Theme Verse

"Let us ... go on to maturity" **(Hebrews 6:1)**.

Goal

To go beyond the very basics, the ABCs of the Christian life, and dig deeply into Scripture while growing in faith and practicing what is learned.

What's Going On Here

Can you imagine how ridiculous it would look if you saw adults walking around in diapers, holding baby rattles in their hands, with pacifiers protruding from their lips? That caricature may describe the spiritual condition of some of those first-century Christians living in the Hebrew community.

That scene may also describe many Christians throughout the ages, including today. Some have spent hours listening to sermons or participating in small-group studies or private devotions. Others have grown lazy about their life in Christ or have rebelled about going beyond the ABCs of the Christian life. They resist spiritual change in their lives.

In some ways we all contribute to what has been called the "confirmation syndrome." With confirmation certificate in hand, we began our spiritual life on milk **(1 Peter 2:2)**. But have we progressed beyond the faith we had as children? Sad to say, even though we may be 40, 50, 60, or older, we may yet be mere youngsters in our Christianity who have not grown in our personal relationship with Jesus. Perhaps we have the correct ("pat") answers and have memorized Scripture in our spiritual childhood. But have we matured spiritually?

As you continue your study of Hebrews, pray that you continue to grow and mature in your faith. Learn what the Lord desires of you.

The writer to the Hebrews showed a very real concern for the spiritual lives of his readers. His thoughts are penetrating! In this section of the book he deals with three areas: immaturity, carelessness, and doubt. But he does this with a spirit of encouragement, not despair!

We see reminders all about us that one day God will call this whole universe to a halt. At that time He will take every believer in Christ to a new, glorious home. While we await that day, God gives us a mission to fulfill—to bring His Gospel to the whole world. Through Word and Sacrament God prepares us for that task.

In today's lesson you will read some words from God about growing toward maturity, overcoming carelessness, and relieving doubts. Perhaps God will use this lesson as a springboard to launch you into a whole new aspect of the Christian life! Ask Him to bless your study.

Searching the Scriptures

1. God expects His children to grow up. Summarize each of the following verses:

a. **1 Corinthians 14:20**

b. **Ephesians 4:14–15**

c. **2 Peter 3:17–18**

What one word summarizes God's desire for your life as described in these verses?

2. The Greek word translated as "slow" in **Hebrews 5:11** is translated as "lazy" in **6:12.** Who is responsible for this condition?

3. God wanted the people to dig deeply into His Word to understand His whole will. What, however, did they need first, according to **5:12?**

4. What is a solution to that problem?

5. Read **Job 32:6–9.** Does age yield wisdom? What does, in fact, give wisdom and maturity?

6. In **Hebrews 5:13–14** the writer seems to be saying that many have remained as children in the protective shelter of the past because they do not put to use what they have learned. What poor habits are implied as contributing to this condition? What other habits can you name?

7. What good habit is mentioned in **5:14?** What is its benefit?

8. Growth to maturity requires us to build on "elementary teachings" **(6:1),** to go beyond always rebuilding the foundation. What ABCs does the writer mention in **verses 1–3?** What teachings do you think God would name today?

9. According to **Hebrews 6:3,** what power gets us out of the nursery and into a growth process?

10. What are some instructions Paul gave to Timothy (**2 Timothy 2:14–19**) for his continued spiritual growth and the growth of those he led?

11. Read **Hebrews 6:4–6.** What tragic end awaits those who, instead of growing and maturing, persist in "crucifying the Son of God all over again and subjecting Him to public disgrace"?

12. What sin is mentioned in **Matthew 12:31–32?** How does this sin disgrace Christ? Why is it not possible to repent and receive forgiveness for this sin? What assurance can you give to those who fear they have committed this sin?

13. What warning does God give in **1 Corinthians 10:12?** Through the means of grace God gives us the power to stand firm. Which means of grace does He mention in **Hebrews 5:11–6:3?**

14. A growing Christian will be a productive Christian (**Hebrews 6:7–9**). Read **John 15:1–5.** How can a Christian be productive?

15. What is the danger of being unproductive?

16. Now read **Ephesians 2:8–10.** What accompanies faith? Why are we able to do them **(2:4–5)?** What benefit can come from them?

17. For what did the writer compliment the people in **Hebrews 6:10?** (See also **10:32–34.**)

18. What encouragement is given in **6:10?** How, according to **verse 11,** are we to make our "hope sure"?

19. Read **Romans 5:3–5.** What advice does Paul offer for tough days?

20. **Hebrews 6:12** encourages Christians to follow the example of those who exhibit mature faith. What two factors help them to persevere?

21. Doubts can be devastating for a Christian. The faith of Abraham is noted in **6:13–15.** Read **Genesis 22:1–18.** How did Abraham show that He trusted in God and believed His promises? How did God deliver Abraham? What was foreshadowed by **Genesis 22:13?**

22. God confirmed His promises by an oath. By whom did God swear that oath? According to **Hebrews 6:18,** why is that oath sure?

23. How does trust in God's promises provide encouragement?

24. The "inner sanctuary" of **Hebrews 6:19–20** is heaven itself. Our hope is described as an anchor moored to Christ. Through the faith Christ gives, we hold onto that anchor. What hope do we now have?

25. Read **Colossians 2:9–12.** How have you been given the sure hope of eternal life with Jesus?

The Word for Us

1. Growing up in our spiritual life is a high priority. It was for the author of Hebrews, too. Growing means more than absorbing the Word of God. It means applying it to your life. In groups of three or four people, discuss ways you can apply the Word and so help one another grow.

2. In your same groups, discuss this statement: "Christians who restrict their intake of the Word will not grow to maturity and therefore may be liabilities to the Christian community." Agree or disagree. Why?

3. Infant Christians act differently from maturing Christians. In your group, try to decide how the immature and the maturing might respond in the following areas:

    a. Digging more deeply into God's Word

    b. Discussing controversial subjects

c. Praying (and the very prayers)

d. Giving of time and money

e. Working in the church

f. Handling confidential information

g. Making judgments and evaluations

4. Sometimes we prefer to just "get by." According to **Hebrews 5:11–6:3,** what do we need in order to get beyond the infant stage and into the growth process?

5. Now individually determine where you are in your Christian growth. Are you stagnating as an infant? barely started growing? having some growth spurts? feeling the growing pains? really growing? having the time of your life growing? What might you do to enhance your growth even more? Make a point of stepping out in a new adventure of Christian life. Don't wait till tomorrow. Do it today!

6. Every church has many different rites and traditions. Although these are helpful in many ways, what can make them "milk" and not "solid food"?

7. What warning do you find in this chapter for anyone who has begun to drift away from a growing life in Jesus? How can you comfort someone who fears he or she has lost all hope of forgiveness?

8. What is needed to heat up the fire of your love for Jesus and a desire to grow up in Him? Where will you find it?

9. Lack of commitment and lack of repentance are two big problems for church members. What are some ways to overcome both?

10. Sometimes we may wonder if God really sees and cares about us personally. What words of **Hebrews 6:10** assure us otherwise?

11. God gives us talents and abilities so that we might reach out to other people. Suggest some ways of using your talents to help others.

12. What comfort can you take in the fact that God never lies?

13. Life with all its difficulties can cause us to become discouraged. What truths from this session will help you overcome discouragement?

14. This section of Scripture has a special message to us especially if we struggle with doubts. What circumstances have caused doubt in your mind? What assurances do you find in this study to relieve those doubts? How can this help you to remain strong even when God doesn't answer your prayers the way you think He should?

Closing

Pray together, **Dear heavenly Father, even though we always intend to serve You and love You, at times we become lazy in our faith growth. We put off things we know we should do. Sometimes we become careless about remaining strong and vigorous in our Christian thoughts and actions. When faced with doubts, we tend to revert to the elementary aspects of Christianity—and to remain there. Forgive us our laziness, our procrastination, our carelessness, our weakness. By the power of Your Spirit, give us the strength and willingness to dig deeply into Your Word so we may exercise our spiritual "muscles." Then guide us as we reach out to others with the Good News we find there. In the name of Jesus Christ, our Savior, we pray. Amen.**

Lesson 6

The Great Melchizedek (Hebrews 7)

Theme Verse

"He is able to save completely those who come to God through Him" (**Hebrews 7:25**).

Goal

To identify the Christian religion as the only true religion because only Jesus is adequate to bring us to God; and, therefore, to desire to live only by the grace of God in Jesus.

What's Going On Here

Who in the world is Melchizedek? We've heard of some of the historical greats of this world: Alexander the Great, Julius Caesar, Christopher Columbus, Abraham Lincoln, Winston Churchill, John Kennedy, William Perry, and a host of others. We hear not only the names but also the many accomplishments of these "greats." But Melchizedek? That's not exactly a household name. In fact, outside of Hebrews, the name is mentioned only twice in the whole Bible. Why does he receive such prominence in this letter to the Hebrew Christians? Is this a mystery cloaked in secrecy that only a Hebrew could understand? Is this a fictitious character invented in order to add some drama? Can it be that he is a figment of the writer's imagination? Or did the writer have a divine purpose for including a man whose name we have difficulty pronouncing (Mel-KIZ-eh-deck)?

David, Abraham, Aaron, Levi, and even Melchizedek were household names to the first readers of this letter. Melchizedek was known and revered from the beginning of Israelite history. Abraham was the first to encounter him. Whether the early believers thought of Abraham (who offered a tithe to him) or David (who wrote a psalm that mentions him) or the writer of Hebrews, it was clear that this great Melchizedek had a whole lot to do with their life with God. For the story of Melchizedek pointed the way to the Son of God, Jesus—who is superior to all and who deserves all honor and glory.

The words of this chapter gave hope to first-century readers who were familiar with Hebrew history. Many of them were suffering, and some had become disillusioned with the way of Jesus. Some had even begun to return to a trust in the Law and the priesthood of former days. They were no longer looking to the Gospel to save them, but to the Law (which could not save them). They needed a strong but loving rebuke followed by an assurance that Jesus is the solution to their needs. He is the High Priest who is greater than the great Melchizedek.

As you begin this study, remember that Jesus is our only help. This lesson logically follows the session on maturing. As we apply this lesson to our daily living, we will be reminded that when things get tough in life, we often revert to the way we did things before. That can tempt us to leave the promises of the Gospel and instead return to a list of "dos" and "don'ts" we learned somewhere in our past. That's a time when we, too, need a strong but loving rebuke and some encouragement to look only to Jesus to help us in our trouble. Remember that fact as you seek to understand the message of this chapter of Hebrews.

Searching the Scriptures

In this chapter the writer speaks of three different priestly lines: Melchizedek, Levi, and Christ.

1. List the qualities of Melchizedek mentioned in **Hebrews 7:1–3.**

a.

b.

c.

d.

e.

f.

g.

(Note that the name "Salem" comes from the Hebrew word *shalom*, which means "peace." "Salem" may have been a shortened form of "Jerusalem," probably the city where he lived.)

2. List the qualities of the priests coming from the line of Levi.

a. **Hebrews 5:1a**

b. **Hebrews 7:28**

c. **Hebrews 5:1b**

d. **Hebrews 5:2b**

e. **Hebrews 7:6**

f. **Hebrews 7:23**

3. List the qualities of the great High Priest, Jesus Christ.

a. **Hebrews 7:14**

b. **Hebrews 7:21**

c. **Hebrews 7:25a**

d. **Hebrews 7:26** (five qualities listed)

e. **Hebrews 7:24**

4. List two reasons why Melchizedek was superior to the priests who came from the line of Levi.

a. **Hebrews 7:4–6a**

b. **Hebrews 7:6b–7**

5. List three reasons why Christ is superior to both Levi and Melchizedek.

a. **Hebrews 7:26**

b. **Hebrews 7:27b**

c. **Hebrews 7:28**

6. Because sin has separated us from God, we need a priest through whom we may approach God. (Sin also prevents us from reaching God without a "go-between.") **Verse 11** makes it clear that the priests of the line of Levi are inadequate to be the "go-betweens." What two reasons in **Hebrews 7:27–28** show that Christ does, in fact, meet that need?

7. The old covenant involved a series of sacrifices offered by human priests. The new covenant is one of pure grace. (We'll get into this more in our next session.) According to **Hebrews 7:21–22** and **27b,** why is the new covenant better?

8. The old covenant with its human priesthood and its system of sacrifices and "dos" and "don'ts" is obsolete. How can we be sure that Christ's priesthood will not also become obsolete, according to **Hebrews 7:24–25?**

9. Jesus lives to intercede for us. Look up the meaning of *intercede* in a dictionary. Now read **1 John 2:1** and **John 16:23–24.** What purposes does Christ's interceding serve?

10. A human priest and human ordinances cannot save us. What words of **verse 27** assure us that Christ can give us eternal life?

11. We need a life that is indestructible. Read **Hebrews 7:16** and **1 Corinthians 15:54–57.** How will we attain an indestructible life?

12. Read **Hebrews 7:18–28** again carefully. List at least two reasons why you will want to trust only Jesus to be your Advocate before God.

The Word for Us

1. "We are all headed for the same place; we just get there by different ways" is a popular belief about heaven. What one thing will keep people out of heaven according to **John 3:18?**

2. Read **John 1:29.** What is the significance of the first *the* in John's statement, "Look, the Lamb of God, who takes away the sin of the world!"?

3. Only God could provide the sacrifice necessary to take away the sins of the world, and only the perfect Lamb of God could be the sacrifice. Read **John 10:30.** How do you know that Jesus is God?

4. Since Jesus is perfect and without sin, He alone can meet our needs. How can God use that knowledge to help us when we are tempted to look elsewhere for spiritual help?

5. Many people raised in a Christian home were also taught a list of "dos" and "don'ts." Have you ever fallen into the trap of believing that if you did what you were supposed to do and didn't do what you weren't supposed to do, God would love you and you could then go to heaven? Why is that kind of thinking and belief inadequate? Why will that kind of thinking lead to a false trust? What is the remedy for such thinking?

6. Looking at **Hebrews 7:18–19,** why is a trust other than in Jesus alone worthless?

7. Sometimes we may think God is not really helping us in our needs. We are expecting more than we are getting. How does **Hebrews 7:26** help us see the picture differently? What further assurance of God's love and help in Jesus do you find in **Philippians 4:19?**

8. We don't earn God's favor by hard work or by striving to please Him. Keeping the Law or offering sacrifices to God will not please Him. Jesus' blood shed on the cross was sufficient payment for our sins. Only the righteousness of Jesus, the great High Priest, which is now ours by grace through faith, makes us presentable to God. What from this lesson will help you remember that life-giving fact?

9. We are invited to pray in Jesus' name. According to **Hebrews 7:25,** why should we do so?

10. When we receive the Lord's Supper, we remember His death until He comes. What do we especially remember?

11. What have you learned during this session that will make you more bold in prayer to God?

Closing

Pray together, **Dear God, just as the first-century Hebrew people struggled between the two covenants—the old, which taught them to offer sacrifices and keep the Law in order to receive Your favor, and the new, which taught that Jesus offered Himself as a sacrifice and kept the Law perfectly in our place, so we also struggle with two different teachings. One lures us with the false promise that if we are good You will love us. The truth is that You have already loved us in Jesus and have done all that is necessary to bring us to You. Give us Your Spirit to help us to remember every day the outstanding truth of the second teaching and to trust only Jesus, our great High Priest, to save us from our sins and to bring us to You. Amen.**

Lesson 7

God's New Arrangement (Hebrews 8)

Theme Verse

"By calling this covenant 'new,' He has made the first one obsolete" (**Hebrews 8:13**).

Goal

To understand that under the new covenant we are completely covered by grace and by grace alone; and to make a new commitment to live for Jesus in this new relationship.

What's Going On Here

The Law that God thundered from Sinai did not set the people free from sin. It did make them more aware of how captive they were to their old nature and how unable they were to keep the Law by their strength. Even so, the people committed themselves to do what the Law required. It provided an external standard of right living. The covenant of the Law was one of "you do" and "I'll do"; everyone was required to obey. Obedience brought blessing, and the disobedient were warned of judgment on their sins.

This old covenant between God and His people served during the time between the Exodus from Egypt and the death and resurrection of Christ. All the while God had a new arrangement in mind.

Under the old covenant the people desiring to be cleansed of their sins counted on the blood that poured from the veins of animals onto the altar as the high priest offered sacrifice for sins. But the effect was never final. The priests again and again had to offer the blood of those creatures slain for the sins of the people. And neither the priest nor the sacrifice was perfect. However, this covenant did point forward to the new one to come—the covenant made through the blood of the new High Priest, Jesus.

The new covenant with its new priesthood did not require a succession of priests. The old ceremonies were made null and void. Now people could live by grace alone and not by works of the Law. In addition, the new covenant would and does free people and allows them to make an internal commitment to live "right side up" in the power of their High Priest, Jesus. This new arrangement is God's covenant of grace, based on none other than Jesus Christ.

What does this mean for you and me? First and foremost, it means we are living under a better—perfect—arrangement of God for His people. We are not waiting for a time when we might enter a new arrangement. We do not depend on models, examples, types, or representations of the real thing. We live in the reality of the present. Christ is real! He has come! He has brought God's new arrangement to us. Therefore, we can look forward to a glorious future with Jesus in heaven. Until then, in the present time, we live with the glorious assurances of the new covenant— assurances that can thrill us! It's a new and wonderful arrangement!

Searching the Scriptures

1. Read **Romans 3:23**. What basic problem makes it necessary for us to have a High Priest seated in the heavens who can plead our forgiveness?

2. Now read **Romans 5:12, 18–19**. How did God deal with the problem?

3. Read about the sacrifices of the old covenant in **Exodus 29:38–46**. How often was it necessary for a priest to offer sacrifice? What blessings did the people thereby receive?

4. Read **Hebrews 10:11–12.** How often did Christ offer His sacrifice? Why, according to **Hebrews 10:14,** is this all that is necessary?

5. Christ came to the heavenly altar with a sacrifice just as an earthly priest always brought an offering to the earthly altar. Read **Hebrews 9:12.** What sacrifice and offering did Christ bring with Him?

6. Read **1 John 1:7.** What benefit do we receive from the sacrifice Christ made?

7. The regular sacrifices offered under the old covenant were only a type, a representation or shadow, of the reality that was to come in Christ. Read **Hebrews 10:3–4.** What purpose did those sacrifices serve? Why were they inadequate for the needs of the people?

8. We humans find it difficult to understand some concepts. Pictures, models, examples, and word pictures help us understand difficult concepts. God commanded Moses to build a replica of the heavenly tabernacle. Read **Exodus 25:8–9, 40** and **Hebrews 8:5.** What did God command Moses concerning the tabernacle? Why?

9. The old covenant was a pledge of loyalty between God (who is ever loyal) and His people. Whose fault was it, according to **Hebrews 8:8,** that the old covenant was replaced?

10. Read **Jeremiah 31:32** and **Hebrews 8:9.** What made the old covenant obsolete?

11. Because it's hard to imagine that anything can be absolutely free, we may have trouble understanding grace. We feel we must do something to earn God's favor. Yet, God's grace is truly free! Read the first sentence of **Hebrews 8:10.** Which words tell you that God is freely giving His grace?

12. The new covenant is one of pure grace—an undeserved free gift. Read **Hebrews 8:10, 12.** What gifts does God promise in His grace? God says:

I will _____ .

I will _____ .

I will _____ .

I will _____ .

I will _____ .

13. Look up **Ephesians 2:8–9.** What does God's grace cost you?

14. The greatest gift we can receive is the forgiveness of sins. What additional promise concerning our sins does God give in **Hebrews 8:12?**

15. What special comfort can we derive from **8:12** concerning our sins and mistakes?

16. The Law with its requirements can never create a loving fellowship. Instead, it accuses us of breaking fellowship with God and our neighbor. Grace assures us that we belong to God's family and have an intimate fellowship with Him. Which words of **8:10** assure you of that?

17. The new covenant of grace also gives power to God's people to know His will and to live in His way. Which words from **8:10** give you that assurance?

18. Read **Colossians 2:20–23.** What words of **verse 23** tell you that the old covenant is powerless to restrain a person?

19. In the new covenant, God's new arrangement, we can take a whole new look at spiritual living. Read **Colossians 3:2–4.** What are you encouraged to do? Why can you now do that? What additional hope is also given?

The Word for Us

The prophecy of Jeremiah quoted in **Hebrews 8:8–12** has been fulfilled in Jesus. We do not anticipate a return to the old covenant. Neither do we anticipate a newer covenant. Therefore we are free to live our lives fully committed to Jesus.

1. As you review what you have learned from **Hebrews 8,** what assurances do you find that the new covenant will last to eternity?

2. What assurances did you find in this lesson that Christ is real (not a shadow of things to come) and that He is forever?

3. Many people living under the old covenant looked forward to the time when the examples, copies, and shadows of the future would become real. We live with reality since Christ has indeed come and is Lord of life. For a moment consider yourself an old covenant person. Why is it easier to believe God now?

4. Since everything necessary for our eternal life has been accomplished in Christ, and since all the shadows and examples of the old covenant have been removed because Christ is All in all, we have no need for objects that resemble the tabernacle in heaven. Yet we use manufactured objects to point us to the reality of heaven and our God. Of what do the following objects remind you?

The building where you worship on Sundays and other times

The altar

The cross

The candlesticks and candles

The sacred vessels (for Communion and Baptism)

The reading and preaching stands

5. What cautions concerning our attitude toward those objects do the words of **Hebrews 8:3–5** suggest?

6. Still today the Law accuses us of sin and tells us just how captive we are to our old nature. How does the new covenant answer that accusation?

7. Under the Law we never receive assurance that our sins have been dealt with completely. What assurances do you have under God's grace?

8. Sometimes we get the feeling that we just "don't measure up" and are not really a part of God's family. Rather, we feel like God is distant and someone to be feared. What does God's grace tell you?

9. Take an inventory of some of your fears. Do they come from a sense that God is going to punish you, a believer, for your sins? When you have committed a sin and are feeling guilty about it, what erases that guilt? Why is it erased? Read **Hebrews 8:12** and memorize it.

10. We often forget that those near and dear to us are also living under grace. How does God's grace enable us to forgive as we have been forgiven? Why are we able to forgive rather than get even?

11. Think for a moment of a way in which someone has sinned against you. How will you forgive that person and forget the sin today?

12. Jesus called disciples of all ages saying, "Come, follow Me" **(Matthew 4:19).** Name some kinds of service you can freely do because you are God's own person by His grace.

13. You can be certain that every day you are, by grace through faith in Jesus, in good standing with God. What can you do to remind yourself of that today?

14. Because you are in good standing, you can, in your desire to live for Jesus, make love of God and love of your neighbor a top priority in your life. How will God's grace give you the strength to do that today?

15. How does God's limitless grace empower you to serve out of love and therefore allow you to give God all the glory?

16. Think for a moment about what life in heaven will be like. Now, jot down a few words of motivation for yourself to live that way today. Remember that the power to do so comes from God!

Closing

Pray together, **Heavenly Father, You have assured us that we are Your own people, called by the name of Christ, forgiven and empowered. Send us Your Spirit to help us live our lives according to Your will so that through our living we may give glory to You. Amen.**

Lesson 8

Once for All ...
(Hebrews 9:1–10:18)

Theme Verse

"He entered the Most Holy Place once for all by His own blood" **(Hebrews 9:12)**.

Goal

That the Holy Spirit may help us to abhor any trust in our own ability to gain a right relationship with God, and also empower us to demonstrate through our daily living and worship a firm trust in the one-time sacrifice of Jesus, so that we may continue to give God thanks for His undeserved mercy and love.

What's Going On Here

The Hebrew lifestyle contained a lot that was exciting and attractive to the senses. Their ancient place of worship was portable and was carried through the wilderness until the vessels and articles used in worship found a permanent home in the temple. When that temple was dedicated and all things were permanently in place, a continued ritual was begun. The regulations for the priests to follow were clear and precise. Rules were followed to the letter. A training program was begun for young members of the tribe of Levi who would serve before the altar of the Lord.

The temple had to be in proper order, and sacrifices had to be offered correctly. The priests would enter regularly into the outer room to carry out their ministry. Morning and evening sacrifices were offered. Once a year, on the Day of Atonement, the high priest would enter the Most Holy Place and sprinkle blood on and before the ark of the covenant.

This ritual was done over and over, year after year (with some interruptions), from the time of the Exodus until A.D. 70, when the temple was destroyed, never to be rebuilt. The Israelites, aware of their history, expected this system to continue forever. They enjoyed the excitement in their worship, especially on the high holy days.

The first-century Hebrew Christians certainly missed the rituals, the temple worship, and all the celebration that accompanied their daily and yearly rites. At times they would long for the old, the familiar, the tangible, and the concrete objects with which they had grown up.

We can understand those people. We, too, have erected our shrines for worship that easily can become shrines to worship. A new congregation is formed and quickly desires to establish its presence in the community. It uses a community building, a school, or even a motel as a temporary place of worship. All of the vessels and articles used for worship must be carried in and out of the temporary place.

The congregation dreams of the day when it will have not only a house of worship, but a building more akin to a cathedral. Ritual, choirs, organs, special music, and singing hold a high priority in the minds of the members as they want to celebrate the goodness of the Lord. Sometimes undue emphasis is placed on the building and the ritual carried on inside it.

This session affirms that our primary emphasis must continually be on the Christ who offered one sacrifice for all time in order to bring all people to God. We need to guard against the tendency to believe that somehow we can add to that sacrifice or that the ritual we use is more important than its object. We need to place our emphasis on Jesus, and thus bring glory to Him.

May our study cause us to look only to the once-for-all sacrifice of Jesus as our source of hope. To assist us, this session is divided into three main sections: a history lesson on blood, a lesson on the benefit of Christ's shed blood, and a lesson on the assurance given to us because Jesus fulfilled the will of the Father.

Searching the Scriptures

1. **Hebrews 9:1–5** summarizes the tabernacle description of **Exodus 25–31** and **35–40**. The tabernacle spoken of was portable and was moved from one location to another. How does this indicate that this form of ritual was only temporary?

2. A permanent home, the temple, was built as a place for sacrifice. Still, the temporary nature of this part of the covenant was indicated through the destruction of the temple in 586 B.C. and the destruction of the rebuilt temple in A.D. 70. How does **Hebrews 9:8** show that the old ritual would be abolished when Christ came?

3. Why, according to **Hebrews 9:9,** were the temple sacrifices in need of replacement by a better sacrifice?

4. **Hebrews 9:10** reminds us of the temporary nature of the old rituals. What are they called? For how long were they to be in effect?

5. **Hebrews 9:11** further emphasizes this point. How do we know that the new tabernacle is perfect?

6. Read **Leviticus 17:11.** In what is life to be found? What makes atonement for one's life?

7. Now read **Hebrews 9:7, 12,** and **22.** Why was blood necessary?

8. Sin is a terrible offense against God. Read **Isaiah 59:2.** What has sin created between you and God?

9. Forgiveness is costly. Read **Hebrews 9:22.** What does it cost for your sins to be forgiven?

10. Both old and new covenants had to be sealed with blood. What, according to **Hebrews 9:16–18,** accompanies the shedding of blood?

11. In **John 1:29** John the Baptizer spoke in prophecy about the forgiveness we would receive through the Christ. Read that verse and also **1 John 1:7.** How can you be sure of forgiveness of all your sins?

12. We cannot solve the internal problem of sin by an external action of our own; nor can we cleanse our conscience by any act we do. Why is this true, according to **Hebrews 9:13–14?** What is God's remedy? What is our response?

13. Read **Hebrews 9:23.** In themselves, heavenly things need no cleansing. We sinful humans, however, would defile them. What was needed for our purification?

14. The high priest entered the Most Holy Place of the tabernacle with blood once each year. According to **Hebrews 9:24–26,** how often would Christ enter the perfect Most Holy Place?

15. What is the purpose of Christ's Second Coming, according to **Hebrews 9:28?**

16. Sacrifices were a reminder of sins committed. The sacrifice of Christ is also a reminder of our sins. What assurance of your forgiveness do you receive in **10:10?**

17. Read **Hebrews 10:13** and **1 Corinthians 15:25–27.** What are the enemies that have become or will become Christ's footstool?

18. Read **Hebrews 10:17–18.** What assurance of God's complete forgiveness do you find there?

The Word for Us

1. Our sin comes to the surface every day. It shows itself in lawless acts. Why, according to **Hebrews 9:9–10,** is it impossible to add anything to Christ's sacrifice for you?

2. When we have sinned, we may hear we have been forgiven, but too often we still live under guilt because we know we have sinned. Our conscience accuses us. What assurances do you find in this lesson to relieve your conscience?

3. Read **Hebrews 9:14** again. How can we demonstrate that we are forgiven?

4. By which acts have you been trying to win God's approval? Read **Hebrews 9:22** again. Why is it impossible to gain favor with God or receive forgiveness of sins through any work we do or any worship we may offer to God?

5. Why do you not need to be afraid of Christ's Second Coming? Who does need to fear the final judgment?

6. Think of a time when you felt you committed a sin that would be hard to forgive—or unforgivable. What words from this section of Hebrews assure you that you have been forgiven?

7. God's Law reminds us of our sin. Why cannot obeying the Law make us acceptable to God?

8. **Hebrews 9:13** uses the word *sanctify*, which means "to set apart for a sacred purpose." For what have you been sanctified?

9. Part of our spiritual life involves participation in rituals or forms of worship. How can these "shadows" lead to "the real thing"—a life of service to Christ?

10. Since you now live under grace and not under the Law, what are some ways in which you can demonstrate your freedom to live for Christ?

11. Since we live under grace and do not have a list of "dos" and "don'ts" by which we try to please God, what is the reason we do attempt to do what God desires?

12. Many hymns remind us that Christ's atonement is forever sufficient to cover our sins. Share one line of a favorite hymn that gives that reminder.

13. Before leaving this lesson on Christ's once-for-all work for you, write down one of the verses from **Hebrews 9:1–10:18** that encourages you to trust Christ only. Now memorize it.

Closing

Pray together, **Heavenly Father, we thank and praise You for sending Your Son, Jesus, as the perfect sacrifice for our sin. We look forward to His glorious return, when He will take each believer to eternal life with You in heaven. We place ourselves at Your disposal so that we might serve You and not ourselves. We pray this in the name of Jesus. Amen.**

Lesson 9

Hang in There
(Hebrews 10:19–39)

Theme Verse

"Do not throw away your confidence" **(Hebrews 10:35)**.

Goal

To continue to grow in confidence in Jesus, seeking His encouragement and discipline in our life so that we may endure all hardship with a living trust in Him.

What's Going On Here

Life can be a real hassle! Anxiety, pressure, and stress are as common as thistles and dandelions. As we go through life attempting to cope with the rock-hard realities of responsibility and accountability, we need effective help to live a Christian life in spite of the difficulties that make us feel like giving up the struggle.

We will find that kind of help in this session. Some of the message will pinch like a too-tight shoe after a couple hours of walking. Some of it will shock us with the high voltage of reality. Most of it will encourage us to "hang in there!" None of it will allow us to opt out of the life God wants His creatures to live.

We'll also find that we have a responsibility not only for ourselves but also for our fellow strugglers in the Christian faith. God doesn't allow a selfish outlook on life. He continually gathers us into a community where we face others who are walking the highway of the called-out life. Sometimes He allows us to suffer hardships. Sometimes we observe others in hardships that range from mild to severe. Always, God reminds us that He is in control, that He is indeed acting in love for the crowning glory of His creation—*us!*

Our God, who is superior to all creatures, holds His loving hands under us and gives us the strength to endure. Jesus Christ is in heaven, where He continues to give us the assurance we need. He reminds us that we truly are His own. He gives the power so that we can endure all hardship. As you study this lesson and apply it to your life, rely on the power of Jesus so that you will "hang in there!"

Searching the Scriptures

1. It seems the author really wanted to make a strong statement when he opened **Hebrews 10:19** with the words *therefore* and *since*. What is that statement? Read **10:19–24.**

2. A first-century Hebrew Christian needed the assurance of these verses. Formerly, anyone other than the high priest entering the Most Holy Place would die instantly. Now, according to **Hebrews 10:19**, how may a Christian approach the Most Holy Place? Why can we have such an attitude?

3. Read **Galatians 3:27.** How have you been prepared to enter the Most Holy Place?

4. Now read **Ephesians 5:25–27.** How has Christ made us fit to enter the Most Holy Place?

5. **Hebrews 10:22** tells us how we, who are His own, should draw near to God. What is the key to that drawing near?

6. **Hebrews 10:23** exhorts us to hang onto the hope given to us. Why are we able to do this?

7. We need encouragement and affirmation. From whom can we expect to receive this, according to **10:24?**

8. Christians are brought into the community of the church. There they are to help one another. We are to worship and fellowship together and to encourage, exhort, and build one another up. According to **10:25,** what is the urgency of this encouragement?

9. **Hebrews 10:26–31** are words of warning. What words of **verse 26** tell you that they are directed to believers?

10. Every Christian is at the same time both a sinner and a saint. Our old nature is sinful and always wants to sin; the new nature created by Jesus is holy, forgiven by God. It wants to be holy, serving God. In **Hebrews 10:26–27,** what punishment does God threaten to people who, despite all

warnings, continue to willfully and deliberately give into the old nature and sin against God and His creatures?

11. According to **10:29,** when we deliberately continue to sin, what are we doing to Christ? to the gracious work of the Holy Spirit?

12. What further warning is given in **10:30–31?**

13. God exhorts us to help one another to grow in our Christian life and to abstain from evil. Read **2 Corinthians 6:14–17.** What is commanded there?

14. In **Hebrews 10:26** God says that if willful sinning continues, no sacrifice for sins is left. Read **Mark 3:29.** What is this kind of sin called? Why will it not be forgiven? (As you think about this sin, recall your discussion of question 12 of "Searching the Scripture" in lesson 5.)

15. The writer to the Hebrews notes several sterling Christian qualities in **10:32–34.** List them.
You stood ...

You were publicly …

You stood side by …

You sympathized …

You joyfully accepted …

16. According to **Hebrews 10:34,** why were the people so faithful?

17. How is the Christian's confidence richly rewarded **(verse 35)?**

18. A Christian who lives in the power of Jesus determines to "hang in there" at all times. How does the writer to the Hebrews say that in **10:39?**

The Word for Us

Hebrews 10:19–39 is not only doctrinal, it is extremely practical. It speaks to each of us about how we are to live our Christian lives, how we are to conduct ourselves in our worship, and how we are to help our fellow Christians remain firm in the faith.

1. Review **Hebrews 10:19–22.** Use simple words to summarize God's invitation. What gives us confidence to accept that invitation?

2. Hope **(verse 23)** grows as we continually look forward to what is coming. Name some means you use to keep yourself looking forward to receiving what God has promised.

3. Satan tempts us to become lazy in our Christian lives **(verse 24).** How can you overcome laziness?

4. If you see a fellow Christian becoming lazy, how might you "spur" that person on? How would you want to be spurred on? In what manner would you receive such an exhortation? Be honest.

5. Missing fellowship opportunities or worship times can easily become a habit **(verse 25).** What are some ways you can encourage your fellow Christians to be more involved in Christian activities and in worship?

6. Our purpose in doing good deeds is to give glory to God. Satan wants us to do them for self-glory or for recognition by others. How can we resist that temptation?

7. Christians can begin to drift away from the Lord and end up so far removed that there is no way back on our own. Who alone can stop the drifting? Whose help is necessary?

8. There is a difference between sins done in ignorance and sins done willfully. What warning do you find in **Hebrews 10:26–31** concerning willful sins?

9. Most of us, enmeshed in bad habits, continue to do things we know are wrong. If that is true of you, spend some time silently
  —speaking a prayer of repentance and
  —resolving, with the help of the Holy Spirit, to stop doing those sins.
You may want to ask a close friend to check up on you. Be open.

10. We live the Christian life day by day by faith in Jesus. Over the long haul this requires endurance **(Hebrews 10:32–39).** The words that follow are related to enduring. Beside each word write a definition to remember when you need encouragement.

Determination

Responsibility

Patience

Diligence

Self-control

11. How will a good, solid foundation in the Christian faith enable you to endure?

12. When others mistreat you because of your faith, what will help you to stand firm?

13. How will you stand firm when the going gets tough and you have pain? suffering? loss of personal goods? heirlooms ruined by a storm? your self-respect assaulted? your God reviled by others? a role reversal or change because of illness or accident?

14. At times we ask the question "why?" when events seem to turn against us. We may wonder, "Why did God do this to me? to us? to our family? to our church?" In light of **Hebrews 10:32–39,** how can you deal with those "why" questions?

15. **Verse 39** states that God strengthens us so that we do not shrink back, but rather believe and are saved. What assures you of that?

16. What are some ways your confidence is boosted? Share them with one another.

17. Write out **Hebrews 10:35–36.** Memorize it and be ready to recall it every time you need to endure.

Closing

Pray together, **Lord, You have called us to a continual life of worship in the arena where we live each day. Thank You for granting Your Son Jesus to open the way for us. Help us to draw near to Him daily in our personal and public worship. Help us always to encourage our fellow Christians to be strong in worship, in acts of love and kindness, and in hope. Forgive us for our sins, especially those we commit willfully, deliberately, and uncaringly. Help us to live in continual repentance and in the strength of Jesus as we live for Him who died and lives for us. In His name we pray. Amen.**

Lesson 10

The Hall of Faith
(Hebrews 11)

Theme Verse

"These were all commended for their faith" **(Hebrews 11:39)**.

Goal

To not just talk about our faith, but also to put that faith into action, as did our ancestors, as we boldly live our lives for Jesus.

What's Going On Here

Hebrews 11 is one of the more exciting chapters in the Bible. The heroes of Scripture are gathered here in the "Hall of Faith." We are introduced to the "greats" of the Old Testament, who remind us to remain strong in faith in Jesus Christ. But, lest we begin to think that only the "greats" of history are included in this hall, we are also introduced to those who remain anonymous. They are included because they endured all things through their trust in God, who had called them into the faith.

Don't forget to put your own name in there as one of the people who belong in the "Hall of Faith." You may have considered yourself too insignificant to be compared with one of the "greats" of Scripture. After all, what you have done hardly compares with Moses holding a rod out over the Red Sea and leading Israel through on dry ground. But don't kid yourself for a minute. By faith you belong in that hall!

Faith is the chief characteristic of the people of God. They live on the promises of God and apply them to their lives in order to know stability and grow to maturity. Heroes don't arrive on the scene full-grown either. They grow up and mature as they exercise their faith. All of their lives are based on their belief in the existence of God, the attributes of God, and His unfailing promises. You can count on this. You, too, are that special person whom God is preparing to enter into that great hall of heaven, where He gathers all those who have believed in Him and have rested on the hope He gives.

So, dive right into this chapter and enjoy it. You are looking at the reality of God Himself, who sustains all of His own. He has never let down anyone who has trusted in Him, so He won't let you down either. So, step into this chapter and then step out with faith in the one true God.

Searching the Scriptures

This session will look at three specific areas of the great teaching of faith to enable us to grow up in the Lord. First, we will talk about what faith is. Next we will look at the faith of our ancestors and see how faith sustained them. Finally, we will look at the everyday workings of faith in the lives of God's people.

1. Read **Hebrews 11:1.** What are three key elements of faith?

2. Read **Hebrews 11:6.** What three elements of faith do you find here?

3. We learn more about faith in **11:39–40.** In this life, we do not necessarily receive what has been promised. When is the end of faith fully realized? Why must it therefore be intertwined with hope?

4. Read **11:13–16** and **Romans 8:24.** How do these passages point out that faith and hope are always involved with the unseen things in this life or the life to come?

5. The unseen has a true existence in the eternal order of things. Agree? Disagree? Why? Read **2 Corinthians 5:7.** How does this passage point out the truth that faith is concerned with the unseen?

6. People have many theories about the origin of the universe. According to **Hebrews 11:3,** what is the explanation for its existence?

7. Write your own definition of faith.

8. Look at the lives of the faithful mentioned in **Hebrews 11.** Tell why each was commended; then tell the results of this person's faith.
   a. Abel **(Genesis 4:1–16)**
   Commended for:

   Result of faith:

   b. Enoch (Genesis 5:21–24)
   Commended for:

   Result of faith:

   c. Noah (Genesis 6:1–9:17)
   Commended for:

   Result of faith:

   d. Abraham **(Genesis 12:1–25:11)** (Note: Abraham was considered to be the father of the Hebrews and therefore much space is allotted to him in **Hebrews 11** in order to show once more that life in Christ is by faith and not by keeping the Law.)
   Commended for:

Result of faith:

Commended for:

Result of faith:

Commended for:

Result of faith:

Commended for:

Result of faith:

e. Isaac **(Genesis 21:1–28:5)**
Commended for:

Result of faith:

f. Jacob **(Genesis 28–49)**
Commended for:

Result of faith:

g. Joseph **(Genesis 37–50)**
Commended for:

Result of faith:

h. Moses' parents **(Exodus 2:1–10)**
Commended for:

Result of faith:

i. Moses **(Exodus 2–14)**
Commended for:

Result of faith:

Commended for:

Result of faith:

Commended for:

Result of faith:

j. Rahab **(Joshua 2; 6:17–25; Matthew 1:5)**
Commended for:

Result of faith:

k. Gideon, Barak, Samson, Jephthah, David, Samuel, the prophets **(Judges; 1 and 2 Samuel, etc.)**
Commended for:

Result of faith:

9. Choose three of these heroes of faith. Briefly reconstruct their lives (Old Testament references to their lives are noted). Share with the class some of the acts of faith you discovered.

10. Christians living by faith in Jesus are not just meek and mild people. Read **Hebrews 11:33–34.** How can we Christians today be strong and conquering, and not passive and weak, for Christ?

11. The Christian life is not free from tragedy. What words of **Hebrews 11:35–38** tell you that?

12. **Hebrews 11:35** speaks of "a better resurrection." What is that resurrection?

13. Go back and reread **Hebrews 10:35–39.** What characteristic describes those who enter the "Hall of Faith"?

14. We don't divide Christians into groups of "supersaints" and "mediocre saints." What one word from **Hebrews 11:39** reminds and assures you that the named and unnamed alike belong in the "Hall of Faith"?

15. The author of Hebrews encourages his readers to endure and be steadfast in their Christian faith to the very end. Write down some verses from **Hebrews 11** that are especially meaningful to you. Memorize them so you will remember them when choices and difficulties come to you.

The Word for Us

1. When you think of an individual of exemplary faith, of whom do you think?

2. Remembering your definition of faith in question 7 above, in which qualities of faith do you need to be strengthened so that you will stand strong? In a prayer ask God to give you these qualities.

3. Have you listened to a child praying lately? What qualities of absolute trust have you noted?

4. We do not want to have a child*ish* faith but a child*like* faith. What qualities of a childlike faith would you like to incorporate into your life?

5. The writer of **Hebrews 11** listed people of great faith. Before these "greats" put their faith into action, they were just ordinary, everyday people of God. What does that tell you about your need to exercise your faith?

6. Many of the "greats" lived without house or permanent home. Instead they were strangers and pilgrims on this earth. What was their permanent home? What is your permanent home?

7. Abraham and Sarah were promised the "impossible." A miracle was necessary for them to have a child. God performed the miracle. What impossible situation is confronting you in your life? Do you believe God is capable and willing to perform a miracle in your life? Do you believe God is still doing miracles today? Why or why not?

8. Walking by faith means you are willing to take the risk to believe that God will come through on His promises. Why do we see so few people willing to take the risk of walking by faith?

9. Only the strong in faith are tested. Agree or disagree? Why?

10. How are you demonstrating to your close friends and your family that faith is confidence in God?

11. What methods would you suggest to overcome the influences that tend to demoralize you and your faith?

12. We are sometimes tempted to panic, to doubt, to complain, or at least to be afraid. Think about Israel crossing the Red Sea. What lesson does God want to teach us about trusting Him to provide the way through every situation?

13. Sometimes God calls us to illogical ways of accomplishing His goals. What do you learn about God's ways from the fall of Jericho's walls?

14. We would like to believe that bad things don't happen to good Christian people. Yet sometimes we see unbelievers experiencing good things and Christians engulfed in tragedies. God commends those who walk by faith in spite of adversity (see **Hebrews 11:35b–38**). Which words of **Hebrews 11:39–40** encourage you to remain faithful no matter what happens?

15. When a friend is suffering illness or other trials, how can you respond to God and to your friend?

16. Life by faith in Christ is more than a secure sitting in the confines of a sanctuary. What response does God teach you in **Hebrews 11?** What promises of **Hebrews 11** help you to live by faith as you venture out for your God?

17. At the end of your life, what has God promised to you? How will you respond when you join with all the other saints in the "Hall of Faith" on that day?

Closing

Pray together, **Father in heaven, thank You for the gift of faith, which You have graciously given us through Your Holy Spirit. Give us the strength to exercise our faith regularly, always remembering our ancestors in the faith. We do not know, nor will we ever know, where You will lead us. We can only go on in faith as did the many "greats" of the past until that day when Christ calls us to Himself in heaven. Until that time give us faith to believe Your promises as we suffer tragedies and enjoy triumphs. Give us Your final blessing—eternal life with You and all Your saints in the "Hall of Faith." Amen.**

Lesson 11

Calm after the Storm (Hebrews 12)

Theme Verse

"Let us run with perseverance the race marked out for us. Let us fix our eyes on Jesus" **(Hebrews 12:1–2).**

Goal

To have confidence that although God must discipline us for our own good, He also provides us with His eternal love to endure the discipline so that in enduring we will finally be given the peace that passes all understanding.

What's Going On Here

Picture a father holding his child close to his breast as he speaks comfortingly and assuringly of his never-ending love for that child. A few minutes earlier the child had acted defiantly and disobediently to his father. Then, with more pain to himself than to the child, the father punished the child. Hurt and disappointed, the child burst into tears. As the sobs subsided, the tender scene described above occurred and we hear the son asking, "Daddy, if you really love me like you say you do, why did you punish me?"

Hebrews 12 helps us understand the Lord's discipline. When God called us to be Christians, He called on us to enter the arena of the Christian life, where there is pain, heartache, hardship, sorrow, setbacks, and even death. We live with a host of forces attempting to defeat us in our life for Christ.

The storms of life are compared to the agony of an athlete in competition for a prize of great worth. Instead of an athletic event, the "competition" revolves around the events of our lives. Like fans at a sporting event, we are encouraged by those in the "Hall of Faith" of **Hebrews 11,** and all those other saints who have gone before. Their example encourages, prods and gives words of hope.

By the grace of God these saints weathered the storms of the Christian life. They pressed on. They endured. The discipline they received worked for their good. Their example says to us, "Endure! Trust your God to give you only the best as you keep your eyes firmly fixed on Jesus. Run the race! Don't drop out! Discipline yourself! Accept every bit of advice that comes from a loving God as He disciplines you. And, keep on running!"

The serene calm—the heavenly peace—comes only after the storm is over. We catch fleeting glimpses of that calm as each storm passes over, but it is never complete until we reach heaven itself.

Searching the Scriptures

Hebrews 12 can be divided into three sections. **Verses 1–3** speak to living in the arena where we contend for the faith; we are given directions on how to endure. **Verses 4–13** encourage us to endure under every kind of heavenly discipline. Finally, **verses 14–29** bring us warnings about living under God's grace, which is absolutely free.

The Arena (12:1–3)

Suppose for a minute that you are standing in the arena receiving directions from the Master for living out your life with endurance.

1. What hinders us **(verse 1)?**

2. What are some entangling sins **(verse 1)?**

3. The race course (the Christian life) has already been laid out. Who laid out the race for us New Testament Christians? How are we to run that race?

4. This race is compared to an athletic event. Read **1 Corinthians 9:24–27.** What methods of preparation for the event does the apostle urge upon us?

5. Read **2 Timothy 2:5.** What further action is necessary for athletes to win the prize?

6. So that we might run to win, **Hebrews 12:2** urges us to "fix our eyes on Jesus." What benefit will that have? (Remember also **3:1.**)

7. Death is an embarrassment, a humiliation that ought not touch us. It is caused by our sin—which causes shame. In taking our shame upon Himself, Jesus dealt with it. What three things does **verse 2** say He did to rid us of our shame?

8. What was "the joy set before Him" **(verse 2)?**

9. What, according to **verse 3,** is the purpose of looking to the endurance of Jesus?

The Discipline (12:4–13)

1. What is the relationship between love and discipline?

2. **Verse 4** speaks of the struggle related to persecutions against the Hebrews. In their struggle these Christians had not yet had their blood shed by their opponents. We know God did not cause the persecution. Nevertheless, how can you tell that God used it as part of His discipline? Read **verses 5–6.**

3. **Verse 5** tells us of two wrong reactions to the Lord's discipline. What are they? Why are they inappropriate for a Christian?

4. When facing discipline, what assurance from **verse 6** can you derive?

5. First-century fathers did not neglect to discipline their children. God still disciplines us as His children. If we are not disciplined by God, what is our condition **(verse 8)?**

6. What is the purpose of God's discipline **(verses 10–11)?**

7. God wills that we endure always, that we may be "healed" (**verse 13**). Think about the picture painted here. Also think back to the cross on Calvary. From where do we draw our healing strength?

Living under Grace (12:14–29)
Here God warns us against worldliness and inattention to His Word.

1. Conflict between people is bound to come about in this sin-filled world. The unchristian element of the world will attempt to infiltrate the church. By the power of God's Spirit, how will we strive for harmony with others?

2. Read **Romans 12:18.** Whose responsibility is it to work toward harmony? Now read **Matthew 5:9.** What promise does Jesus give those who seek harmony?

3. **Hebrews 12:15** encourages us to live by the free grace of God. How can that overcome the temptation to be legalistic, rigid, and demanding in one's faith-life?

4. Bitterness, like a root, grows below the surface. What happens when we allow bitterness to get rooted and start growing?

5. Think of our sexually permissive society. What warning is given in **verse 16a?** (See also **Matthew 5:8.**) Where do you get the strength to remain pure?

6. What lesson do you learn from the example of Esau's selling everything for a moment of pleasure **(verse 16b)?**

7. God's law **(verses 18–21, 26–27)** creates a real storm of fear, gloom, and darkness. **Verse 29** adds that God is a consuming fire. All this reminds us that God is holy. Which word in **verse 18,** however, is very comforting?

8. Explain the contrast between Mount Sinai **(12:18–21)** and Mount Zion **(12:22–24).** Describe the joy that is yours because "you have come to Mount Zion" **(verse 22).**

9. Once more, there will be a storm when God destroys this whole creation at the Last Day. What assurance do you have **(verse 28)** that you will have a calm after the storm?

The Word for Us

1. To live the Christian life takes continual training. We must get rid of the "flab" in our lives. Although not sinful in themselves, some societal, business, or personal associations and engagements must be eliminated. Why?

2. What are several factors that can increase your confidence as you run the race of the Christian life?

3. When we have the attitude of Jesus, we will run the race to its completion. But we can't get that attitude on our own. How can we get it?

4. Notice the first words of **Hebrews 12:1.** How will reflection on the heroes of **chapter 11** help you to run the race with patience and endurance?

5. Name and discuss some ways you might be a "cheering section" for some of your fellow runners.

6. Recall some of the discipline you received from your parents. Share one incident when affection, affirmation, and help was given along with necessary discipline.

7. We have no guarantee that we will not encounter persecution. What "exercise" or methods do you use to discipline yourself to continue to endure persecution and to live your Christian life to the fullest? Share your thoughts and ask others to help you.

8. Thinking of the message in this chapter, what is a purpose of some of the suffering in the lives of Christians?

9. Name some ways you might help others to live a more disciplined life.

10. Christians living in some parts of this world are suffering for their faith and yet remain strong and vibrant in their Christian lives. What reasons could you give for this?

11. Why should you not fight, resist, or resent discipline?

12. When we experience difficulty as a result of another person's actions, we often react by fighting back. How can we overcome that temptation? Name some ways of pursuing peace with your fellow Christians.

13. Unless resentment is overcome, bitterness may take root. It may be against employers, friends, family, teachers, pastors, and others. How can you overcome resentment and cut out the root of bitterness before it causes poisonous problems?

14. Name some ways you can resist impurity in life.

15. Sometimes we are tempted to make up our own "shoulds" and "should nots" rather than to live purely by the grace of God. Why is it unnecessary and harmful to make up rules for running the race?

Closing

Pray together, **Dear Father in heaven, running the Christian race is arduous. It takes training. It takes discipline from You. It takes self-discipline. Sometimes we resent Your discipline or the pain involved in the process. Yet we know that behind it is Your love and Your desire that we persevere in the race You have laid out for us. Thank You for Your Word, which encourages us. Thank You for Your sacraments, which strengthen us. Thank You for the assurance that, as we keep our eyes firmly fixed on Jesus, we will overcome and obtain the victory; by Your love and through the forgiving blood of Jesus, we will reach the other side of the storm and there experience an eternal calm with You. Amen.**

Lesson 12

Remembering
Whose You Are
(Hebrews 13)

Theme Verse

"May the God of peace, who through the blood of the eternal covenant brought back from the dead our Lord Jesus, that great Shepherd of the sheep, equip you with everything good for doing His will, and may He work in us what is pleasing to Him, through Jesus Christ, to whom be glory for ever and ever. Amen" **(Hebrews 13:20–21)**.

Goal

That, by the power of the Spirit, we may remain pure and grow in love and respect for all; give honor to all leaders whom God has given; and serve the Lord with a willing spirit.

What's Going On Here

Do you need some straight, practical advice for living under the Son? If so, rejoice. God provides such exhortation in the final words of the letter you have been privileged to study. The advice is personal. It is caring. It brings us face-to-face with a number of issues we may have been evading because of the trends in our society. It calls for involvement in the life of this world with a total commitment to the life of Christ. And it comes in the context of the grace that provides the only source of strength by which we can live this life.

We sometimes take the easy way out and live our Christianity within the walls of our own lives, homes, and churches. Things often seem more comfortable and less demanding there. But we are tempted to neglect some of the points of the Christian life that will give a firm, strong witness to those outside the church.

The writer to the Hebrews recognized that we exhibit our Christianity to the world about us by the way we live our lives in the church and in the world. He first speaks about the way we act toward one another. Next he gives advice about living our married or single lives and speaks to our fascination with riches and possessions. Finally, he discusses our respect for and love to our leaders in the Lord.

Without a doubt, Christians throughout the ages have struggled with living life in a way that honors our Lord. The writer here encourages us to continue the struggle with confidence in Christ and to make our faith in Him obvious by our service in His church.

What our Lord Jesus commands, He also enables. We know that in His grace He will give us the strength to be a community of people who display His character. That's a tough assignment! But, as we undertake this, we can be certain that He will empower us to live up to the example He has set for us. We dare not rely on our own wisdom, for in our weakness we would fail. We must look to Jesus! We must rely on Jesus! He will give us all we need!

What a fitting way to conclude this book! These 13 chapters of Hebrews are filled with truth for our living. Now let's take it to heart. Let's let that powerful Word of God work in us so that we glorify Him by our lives. Review these words often. In fact, why not set aside a time each year to savor again the truth of this book. And then, by His power, determine to live your life to the fullest under Jesus Christ, the Fulfillment of Faith!

Searching the Scriptures

1. As we read **Hebrews 13,** we need to remember its context within the entire letter. Thus, we know that the brotherly love in **verse 1** is inspired by the love of Christ to us. A first-century Hebrew Christian would understand loving Hebrew brothers as a national duty. Why is the love spoken of here free from national, racial, or creedal boundaries?

2. God desires love not only to brothers and sisters in the Lord, but also to strangers. Abraham **(Genesis 18:1–15)** entertained angels unaware. What reason, besides the command in **verse 2,** do we have for treating strangers with compassion and love?

3. **Hebrews 13:3** seems to be a "golden rule" statement—"do to others what you would have them do to you." Read **Matthew 25:34–40** (especially **verse 40**). How can you tell that such action is on a higher level than even the "golden rule"?

4. Infidelity results when people are indifferent to sexual purity and when they compromise God's high ideals for both married and single persons. How can we possibly expect two people to bind themselves together until death?

5. Read **Hebrews 13:5** and **1 Timothy 6:10.** How can possessions or money lead to sin?

6. Read **Philippians 4:19.** Of what can we be sure?

7. Remembering God's promises will help us keep our lives in perspective. What special promise do you find in **Deuteronomy 31:6, 8; Joshua 1:5; Matthew 28:20;** and **Hebrews 13:5?**

8. Each day we need courage to live our Christian life, because we will certainly be tested by the world around us. What promises for those times do you find in **Psalm 118:6–7** and **Hebrews 13:6?**

9. **Verses 7** and **17** speak of duties toward our leaders in the Lord. In which ways, according to this verse, are we to give honor to them? Give an example of each.

10. Why, according to **verse 17,** do leaders need your obedience?

11. **Verse 8** speaks of Jesus as being utterly consistent. How can this truth help you to keep imitating the faith of leaders and giving them your wholehearted support?

12. First-century Hebrew Christians were often tempted to return to some of the former worship ceremonies or to live a way of life that had teachings contrary to Christianity. That's a problem for us, too. Read

2 Timothy 4:3–4. What happens to people who pay attention to those false teachings? According to **Hebrews 13:9,** what provides the strength to resist those false teachings?

13. The altar of **verse 10** is obviously the Lord's altar and not the temple or tabernacle altar. Why is our altar better?

14. Religious systems, orders of worship, and earthly shrines will not last. They are limited to customs, cultures, and locations. But they have a way of entrapping us. **Verses 11–14** encourage us to look elsewhere for that which is unlimited and eternal. What do we look for? Where is it located? What may we have to endure if we dare to look beyond the present, limiting systems that people may develop?

15. God exhorts us to make sacrifices to Him—not to gain His favor, but to give Him honor and glory. What are four of those sacrifices **(verses 15–16)?** Give a concrete example of each one.

16. How does God feel about sacrifices given out of a good and true heart?

17. The writer to the Hebrews asked his readers specifically (as opposed to generally) to pray for him **(verses 18–19).** What was the specific need?

18. In **verses 20–21** the writer sums up all that the letter contains and puts it into the form of a fervent prayer-wish, or benediction, for the first readers and for you. What thoughts go through your mind as you read that prayer?

19. In a postscript **(verses 22–25)** we receive encouragement to greet one another. The writer's greetings include good news of Timothy, Paul's spiritual "son" **(1 Timothy 1:18),** to whom that apostle addressed two letters. How can such greetings encourage you and others?

The Word for Us

1. Some people are easier to love than others. What one factor about brothers and sisters in the Lord will help you to show love to all Christians everywhere?

2. When we reach out to touch the lives of others, especially strangers, we risk being misunderstood or even rejected. What helps us to be willing to take that risk?

3. Some fellow Christians are imprisoned—not by bars but by circumstances. How can you be reminded often to make the effort to reach out to them also? How can you help one another "spot" these people in your midst?

4. God's teaching on sexual purity is strict but of great importance. God originated the relationship of marriage and offers His grace to maintain it. What are some actions you can take to guard that relationship and to fulfill or help others fulfill it according to His will?

5. God judges those who continue in impure sexual living. When a person caught in impurity is repentant, how can you help that person to have his or her life restored?

6. So often we are tempted to "keep up with the Joneses." Read **Philippians 4:12.** How did Paul answer the question, "How can I deal with financial concerns?"

7. Fear causes us to want to accumulate more and more and so increase our sense of security. Why is this like "chasing after the wind" **(Ecclesiastes 2:11)?**

8. What role will humility play for us as we attempt to live within our means and seek satisfaction in God rather than in possessions?

9. Opinion is like a hurricane: unpredictable in its course and deadly when it strikes. All people, especially leaders, are subject to the storm of public opinion. How can the words of **Hebrews 13:6** help us overcome the torrents of people's opinions about us and our faith-life?

10. When we observe our leaders (in church and civil government), we can easily concentrate on their flaws and weaknesses. We need to remember that our God-appointed leaders have positions of authority in spite of their weaknesses. What do we owe to our government leaders? to our church officials? to our pastor?

11. Pastors carry a special burden for the people under their charge. Name some ways we can help to make their work a joy, their burden lighter.

12. Sometimes we need to swallow our pride as we follow our God-appointed leaders. Why is that necessary?

13. What are some questions you have about following God's leaders? Discuss them in your study group.

14. Human teachings can sometimes look like the "real thing" of God's teachings found in the Bible. What is one factor that will tell us whether a religious organization is Christian or non-Christian? (Look at **Hebrews 13:9** and compare "foods" with "grace.") Discuss some of the religious organizations in your community. How can we tell if they are Christian?

15. Standing up for Jesus and the truth of the Bible will sometimes bring us trouble. What encouragement to stand strong do you find in **Hebrews 13:13–14?** What encouragement could you give to a fellow Christian?

16. One excellent way to express our praise to the Lord is to sing! What is one of your favorite spiritual songs? If possible, sing some of those favorites now.

17. Follow the example of the writer to the Hebrews **(verses 18–19)**. Ask someone in your group to pray for one of your needs. Stop now to pray.

18. As you review **verses 21–25,** take a minute to greet one another and to speak a benediction or blessing to one another. Write a benediction in your next letter to a friend.

Closing

Pray together, **Heavenly Father, we thank You for the opportunity we have had to study Your Word together. We ask Your Holy Spirit to be present in our lives as we now put this learning into action. Be with us, we pray, so that we may always be faithful to You in every aspect of our lives. We remember all our leaders in prayer— governmental, civil, employment, and spiritual leaders. Give them all Your wisdom and discernment as they guide us. Enter into the hearts of those leaders who do not know You. Also help us to remember one another in prayer, especially now that class is over. Guide us with Your grace until that day when we finally see You face-to-face. All this we pray in the name of Your Son, Jesus. Amen.**

HEBREWS

The Fulfillment of Faith

Leaders Notes

Leaders Notes

Preparing to Teach Hebrews

Congratulations! You have been chosen to be the leader (or one of several leaders) in a study of one of the most exciting and instructive books of the Bible! Surely you and those with whom you work will profit greatly by this study as you grow in love for your Lord Jesus and in knowing His will for your lives. These Leaders Notes have been prepared to help you lead a group through Hebrews. Directions are provided for suggested conduct of the class; insights into some of the ideas, concepts, and idioms of the time and place of the book; and suggestions to help your group come out of each lesson with appropriate conclusions.

You do not need to be a lecturer to lead this study. You are a facilitator—helping others to understand how God's Word impacts their lives. You need not do all the research or all the talking. Consult some quality commentaries such as the *Concordia Self-Study Commentary* (CPH, 1979) and the *People's Bible Commentary on Hebrews* (CPH, 1992) as you prepare for each lesson. Also read the text in a modern translation. The NIV is referred to in the lesson comments. But most of all, depend on the Holy Spirit to guide you in your preparation and leading. May God bless you and those you lead!

Group Bible Study

Group Bible study means mutual learning from one another under the guidance of a leader or facilitator. The Bible is an inexhaustible resource. No one person can discover all it has to offer. In a class many eyes see many things and can apply them to many life situations. The leader should resist the temptation to "give the answers" and to act as an "authority." This teaching approach stifles participation by individual members and can actually hamper learning. As a general rule the teacher is not to "give interpretation" but to "develop interpreters." Of course, there are times when the leader should and must share insights and information gained by his or her own deeper research. The ideal class is one in which the leader guides class members through the lesson and engages them in meaningful sharing and discussion at all points, leading them to a summary of the lesson at the close. As a general rule, don't tell the learners what they can discover by themselves.

The general aim of every Bible study is to help people grow spiritually, not merely in biblical and theological knowledge, but also in Christian thinking and living. This means growth in Christian attitudes, insights, and skills for Christian living. The focus of this course must be the church and the world of our day. The guiding question will be, What does the Lord teach us for life today through the book of Hebrews?

Pace Your Teaching

Do not try to cover every question in each lesson. This attempt would lead to undue haste and frustration. Be selective. Pace your teaching. Spend no more than five minutes with the "Theme Verse" and "Goal" and two or three minutes with "What's Going On Here." Allow 20 minutes to apply the lesson ("The Word for Us") and five minutes for "Closing." This schedule, you will notice, allows only about 30 minutes for working with the text ("Searching the Scriptures").

Should your group have more than a one-hour class period, you can take it more leisurely. But do not allow any lesson to "drag" and become tiresome. Keep it moving. Keep it alive. Keep it deeply meaningful. Eliminate some questions and restrict yourself to those questions most meaningful to the members of the class. If most members study the text at home, they can report their findings, and the time gained can be applied to relating the lesson to life.

Good Preparation

Good preparation by the leader usually affects the pleasure and satisfaction the class will experience.

Suggestions to the Leader for Using the Study Guide

The Lesson Pattern

The material in this guide is designed to aid *Bible study*, that is, a consideration of the written Word of God, with discussion and personal application growing out of the text at hand. The typical lesson is divided into these sections:

1. Theme Verse
2. Goal
3. What's Going On Here
4. Searching the Scriptures
5. The Word for Us
6. Closing

"Theme Verse" and "Goal" give the leader assistance in arousing the interest of the group in the concepts of the lesson. In these notes for you, the leader, these two sections are covered under "Getting Started" because that is their purpose: to get the learners to start thinking about the lesson. Do not linger too long over the introductory remarks. Use them merely to show that the material to be studied is meaningful to Christian faith and life today.

"What's Going On Here" helps you gain an understanding of the textual portion to be considered in the session. Before the text is broken down for closer scrutiny, it should be seen in the perspective of a greater whole. At this point the class leader takes the participants to a higher elevation to show them the general layout of the lesson. The overview gives the group an idea where it is going, what individual places are to be visited, and how the two are interrelated.

"Searching the Scriptures" provides the real "spadework" necessary for Bible study. Here the class digs, uncovers, and discovers; it gets the facts and observes them. Comment from the leader is needed only to the extent that it helps the group understand the text. The questions in the Study Guide are intended to help the learners discover the meaning of the text. Having determined what the text says, the class is ready to apply the message. Having heard, read, marked, and learned the Word of God, we proceed to digest it inwardly through discussion, evaluation, and application. This is done, as the Study Guide suggests, by taking the truths of Hebrews and applying them to the world and Christianity in general and then to personal Christian life. Class time may not permit discussion of all the questions and topics.

Remember, the Word of God is sacred, but the Study Guide is not. The guide offers only suggestions. The leader should not hesitate to alter the guidelines or substitute others to meet his or her needs and the needs of the participants. Adapt your teaching plan to your class and your class period. Good teaching directs the learner to discover for himself or herself. For the teacher this means directing the learner, not giving the learner answers. Choose the verses that should be looked up in Scripture. What discussion questions will you ask? At what points? Write them in the margin of your Study Guide. Involve class members, but give them clear directions.

Begin the class time with prayer, and allow time for brief closing devotions at the end of the class session. Suggestions for brief closing devotions are given in the Study Guide. Remember to pray frequently outside of class for yourself and your class. May God the Holy Spirit bless your study and your leading of others into the comforting truths of God's Christ-centered Word.

Lesson 1
Focus on the Son (Hebrews 1)

Before the Session
Begin your preparation well-ahead of the first class session by reading through the entire book of Hebrews. Highlight verses or sections that pique your interest. Use a commentary to help explain any questions about what the author is saying. Your class will be looking to you as a resource person, but don't think that you have to know all the answers. Search together as a class for an answer, but don't be afraid to admit that you don't know an answer—there are some things that only God knows.

Before every class session, make sure that your meeting room is ready; that the temperature is comfortable, that there are enough tables and chairs, and that there are extra pencils and Bibles available for participants.

Getting Started
You are beginning a study of a most exciting and inspirational Bible book. What better place to begin than with a firsthand look at the most exciting person in history—Jesus Christ! Before proceeding with the study, have the class talk among themselves first in pairs and then in a large group about what they want to learn from this Bible study. Not only will this activity set some goals for you, it will also help participants get to know one another.

Then ask the class to read the introduction to Hebrews printed in the Study Guide. Knowing the historical background of the early Christians will help to give insight to the study of Hebrews. It will be helpful if 20th-century people can see that Christians of all times have had to deal with difficulties even as they enjoyed the radiance of God's love in Jesus. Be sure to emphasize that it is only in Jesus that Christians of all times have been able to find hope.

The Class Session
Have a volunteer read "What's Going on Here" to introduce the session. It should be self-explanatory, but if some questions arise, take time to respond to them. Do not spend an inordinate amount of time on this, since many questions will be answered through the study of the Word. If you need additional historical information, quickly look for it in a commentary or have a volunteer search for this information before the next class period.

Searching the Scriptures

These Leaders Notes are designed to provide answers to most Study Guide questions. It does not, however, provide answers when they seem very obvious or when the question is designed to promote discussion that involves personal opinions.

1. Many discussion leaders fear silence, but silence is necessary at times to give participants time to think about the question or issue being raised. Occasionally you may actually want to time the silence before asking for an oral response. Fifteen seconds, for example, may seem like a long time, but participants may need that much time to think through a question. For the seven answers for this question, you might allow at least two minutes—or more—if participants are still writing at the end of that time.

Encourage participants to write these answers, but do *not* insist on it. People generally are more willing to get involved in a discussion if they feel comfortable with the instructions you provide. Do not try to force them to respond in ways that seem to upset them.

a. "appointed heir of all things"

b. "through whom He made the universe"

c. "the radiance of God's glory"

d. "the exact representation of His being"

e. "sustaining all things by His powerful word"

f. "provided purification for sins"

g. "He sat down at the right hand of the Majesty in heaven"

2. Jesus and the Father are one, the Father in Jesus and He in the Father—a unity.

3. By faith we know that Jesus is doing all the things the Father does.

4. "You are My Son; today I have become Your Father." "Sit at My right hand."

5. God tells us to worship only Him and His Son, Jesus.

6. The writer shows the "God-ness" of Jesus as follows:

verse 8—"Your throne, O God, will last for ever ... righteousness will be the scepter."

verse 9—"God ... has set You above Your companions by anointing You."

verse 10—"You laid the foundations of the earth, and the heavens are the work of Your hands."

verses 11–12—"You remain ... Your years will never end."

verses 13–14—"Sit at My right hand."

7. Questions 99–100 of the 1986 exposition of Luther's Small Catechism provide additional information about angels. Answers for the Study Guide references should be self-evident.

8. Angels serve believers, who are on their way to heaven.

9. Expect answers such as protect us, serve us, warn us about danger.

10. The author writes, "Your throne, O God, will last for ever **(verse 8)** and "Are not all angels ministering spirits?" **(verse 14).**

11. Angels are servants sent by Jesus to serve those for whom He died.

12. Jesus is Creator, eternal, almighty, and changeless.

13. Encourage volunteers to describe the Jesus they have seen. Note the many different ways people describe Jesus.

The Word for Us

1. God does not reveal divine truth to us outside of the Bible. Any truth revealed must have its base in Scripture, which is the last Word God has given to this present world.

2. Emphasize that it's almost always foolish to argue about questions like this one. Probably a better strategy would be to simply point to **Hebrews 1:1–2,** which says that in Jesus God has given us His final revelation. Also you may want to point out that sometimes when people say that God spoke to them, they really mean that some Word of the Bible became clear to them for the first time.

3–5. Invite volunteers to respond to these questions or, at times, allow 5–10 seconds of silence for personal reflection.

6. God certainly encourages us to turn to Jesus during difficulties!

7. Point out the assurance we find in **verses 10–12.**

8. Recall for your group the discussion you had in connection with questions 7–9 in the previous section. Then encourage participants to suggest other things angels may do for them.

9. Angels cannot save us, give us forgiveness, or give us eternal life.

10. Answers will vary. Look for praise words like *holy, changeless,* and *ever-present.*

Closing

Pray that, as a result of this study, God will have led you and the participants to conclude that

a. the Bible is God's Word, His last word given to this world;

b. Jesus is not only the Son of God, but is in every way God;

c. while we are living by faith in this world, we do not focus only on a "God figure" but on *Jesus,* and we become very specific in our references to God (i.e., Father, Jesus, Holy Spirit).

With this in mind pray with the participants the prayer in the Study Guide. Then encourage all to read **Hebrews 2** and to begin to work through the questions in lesson 2 of the Study Guide.

Lesson 2

It's All in the Way You Look at It (Hebrews 2)

Before the Session

Read **Hebrews 2.** Also read **Leviticus 16** for a description of the clothes and duties of the high priest.

Getting Started

Have the group talk about suffering: What forms does it take? Does it have a purpose? Is it ever good? Is anyone ever exempt? Your group will probably agree that they all wish suffering would go away. That joy, however, must wait until heaven. Meanwhile, we live in a world in which Satan still causes all kinds of pain and suffering. The good news for this session is that God works through pain and suffering to increase our faith and thus to crown us with glory and honor, just as He crowned His Son with glory and honor when He suffered death for us **(Hebrews 2:9).** God also gives us the power to endure and, thus, to receive the crown of eternal life.

The Class Session

Begin with a prayer asking God to give you insight into His suffering and strength to endure your suffering. Then have volunteers read the "Theme Verse" and "Goal." Ask someone who reads with emphasis to read aloud "What's Going On Here." This Study Guide section probably will evoke some emotion in the participants. Expect some questions or comments that indicate that some participants may not be tuned in to suffering. Don't belabor the point, but you might note that not all Christians in the world live as comfortably as most of us in America.

Searching the Scriptures

This section covers three distinct areas: a warning against falling away from the Lord through the neglect of His Word; an emphasis on the person of Jesus and His suffering and death to earn forgiveness for our sins; and the assurance that temptations can be overcome through Jesus.

Discuss these questions with the entire group. If the group is large, however, you might occasionally ask small groups to discuss them first. This process can help get everyone involved.

1. God's Word is binding on all of us, violation of God's Word will be punished, God's Word is completely trustworthy, and God continues to give His help by His Holy Spirit. Be sure to emphasize that last point.

Although we may want to remain steadfast, any attempt to do this by our own power plays right into Satan's hands and will, therefore, surely end in failure. But when we depend on God instead of ourselves, and look to His Word and sacraments for faith food, we can be sure He will keep us faithful until death.

2. Volunteers may mention all the sins listed in **2 Timothy 3:1–9.** A good summary word is *disobedience.* Participants may also note that too much emphasis on self will cause one to drift and fall away.

3. Through the Bible God will teach, rebuke, correct, and train us, and He will equip us to remain faithful and to do His work.

4. To reject God's admonition and exhortation is to reject God and thus receive eternal punishment.

5. Answers will vary. Look for such answers as rumors, personal hurts, anger, selfishness, family breakup, sexually transmitted diseases, disregard for others, and desire to get rather than to give.

6. If time allows, you might discuss how God used New Testament writers to bring out the eschatological (end-of-the-world) implications of words that seem nonprophetic. Note that **Hebrews 2:9** applies the words of **Psalm 8:4–6** to Jesus. Emphasize the joy that God offers us because we have the fullness of His message. God gave us humans authority over created beings and the earth. He gave His Son authority over everything in heaven and on earth. Jesus has all glory and honor.

7. Jesus forgives our wrongs and gives help, strength, and wisdom. In God's Word we learn what pleases Him.

8. Jesus gave His life for us. He was our substitute. He suffered death in our place. Note the motivation for this saving act: God's grace. Our death could not atone for our sin.

9. You might invite participants to scan **1 Corinthians 15:20–58** and read aloud verses or thoughts that are especially meaningful to them. Through His resurrection Jesus conquered death.

10. Invite participants to contrast Jesus' path to glory (obedience, suffering, and death) with the path we humans often follow when we seek glory.

11. Because Christ took sin's punishment on our behalf, we and all who believe in Him will never be punished for our sins. He promised that He would raise us all from death by the power of His own resurrection.

12. **Hebrews 2:14–18** clearly points out the blessings we enjoy because Jesus became (and remains) human. He destroyed the power of Satan, freed us from punishment, won our forgiveness, and calls us children (Abraham's descendants). He has paid the total price for us and will not hold our sin against us.

13. Satan tempted Jesus to serve self, to test God, and to worship the tempter.

14. Answers could include temptations to power, to grandeur, to self-glory, to judge others, to deal in anger, or even to take the easy way out (such as in Gethsemane). Jesus faced every temptation that we face today.

15. Jesus suffered our temptations—and won. Note that when He entered the state of exaltation, Jesus kept His humanity. He *is* our faithful High Priest. He *is* able to help us when we are tempted. In a very real way we can go to Him for strength to help us overcome temptation.

The Word for Us

You may want to encourage people to work in pairs or triads on the first four questions in this section.

1. Most Christians waver between reliance on self and God. **Proverbs 3:1–5** encourages us to trust *only* the Lord.

2. God empowers us to rely on Him when we remember whose we are, recall His Word, and stop to think about that Word before we act.

3. If the class has worked in pairs or triads, ask volunteers to share their suggestions.

4. Though perfectly innocent, Jesus died for the guilty. For His sake God has declared us innocent. Through His intercession for our sins, He continues to help us today.

5. By God's grace we, the forgiven, forgive others. Jesus helps us remember this through His words, "Forgive us our sins, for we also forgive everyone who sins against us" (**Luke 11:4;** these words are part of the Lord's Prayer). The power He gives through such forgiveness enables us to follow that command.

6. All who have died in Jesus will certainly enter into glory with Him.

7. Amid suffering God brings us blessings when He causes us to recognize the folly of trusting in our own goodness. He brings the richest blessings (life in God's kingdom here on earth and, finally, in heaven) when He empowers us to trust in Him as the only one who can deliver us.

8. God's Spirit living within us can cause us to consider material things as unimportant, focus on the cross of Jesus, live for Him (by His strength), look forward to the resurrection, etc.

9. Many have a nagging guilt about a sin done in the past. Help each to see that we become a slave to that sin when we allow it to remain in our thoughts by failing to confess it and to receive Jesus' forgiveness. Jesus has covered, forgiven, and forgotten our sin and freed us from the slavery of sin!

10. Participants may suggest that when they have suffered, they know

what it feels like and would not want others to suffer in the same way; if someone is suffering, we feel for and with that person.

Closing

Pray that, as a result of this study, God will have led you and the participants to conclude that

a. we show love to others when we warn them about becoming lax in their faith, because we want them to be saved;

b. Christ has undergone total suffering for us and has forgiven every sin and removed all guilt;

c. Jesus is our constant Help. He not only forgives the past, but He assists us in the present to resist temptations.

Keep this in mind as you pray with the participants the prayer in the Study Guide. Then encourage all to read **Hebrews 3:1–4:13** and to begin to work through the questions in lesson 3 of the Study Guide.

Lesson 3

Don't Miss Out on the Rest (Hebrews 3:1–4:13)

Before the Session

Read **Hebrews 3:1–4:13,** marking notes of interest and questions. Review the life of Moses and the exodus **(Exodus 2–20).**

Getting Started

As people arrive, have them write down and then share some of the dangers that arise when people become complacent in their faith. As they share, urge participants to encourage one another to be and remain faithful to a most faithful God.

The Class Session

Have a volunteer read the "Theme Verse" and "Goal." Share with the participants that **Hebrews 3** contains one of the sternest warnings of the entire book. This session is designed to help each person examine his or her own life with the Lord and develop a renewed zeal for living the Christian life.

Have another volunteer read "What's Going On Here." Notice that the text moves from talking about physical rest to spiritual rest. At times we become lax in our Christian lives. Then we need to be exhorted to remain alert at all times and never take the grace of God for granted by becoming slipshod in our lives. Ask participants to share some of the ways we, who are accustomed to having an easy church life, could possibly slip into disbelief or even unbelief. Don't spend a lot of time on it, but do allow at least a few minutes for this exercise.

Searching the Scriptures

The questions will lead participants through **Hebrews 3:1–4:13** and into related Old and New Testament verses. One word will stand out—*encouragement*. Christian love motivates us to help and encourage one another.

1. Perseverance—holding on to our courage and hope—is a hallmark of a child of God. Failure to persevere endangers spiritual life.

2. God requires that we prove ourselves faithful with those things entrusted to us. As in the previous question, this is not a means by which we earn His favor, but a mark that shows God is active in our lives.

3. God reminds us to fix our thoughts on Jesus, (i.e., to keep Him uppermost in our thoughts and minds). We can do this because of God's power living in us. He gives us a living hope, promises for the future, and protection of our faith. (We cannot create faith in ourselves; that is the work of God. However, He does not take faith away from us. That happens through our own turning away.)

4. Unless questions arise, work through this section rather quickly. Just give enough background so everyone understands what the writer is saying in **Hebrews 3:7–19.** In **Exodus 17:1–7** we see that

a. the people's faith that God would provide all that was needed for their lives was tested;

b. the people grumbled against Moses, questioned whether God was with them, and quarreled;

c. the people sinned by testing the Lord with unbelief;

d. the place was named Massah ("testing") and Meribah ("rebellion" or "quarreling") to remind them of their sin;

e. the people should have learned that God will take care of His children.

In **Numbers 13:1–14:4** we see that

a. Israel's trust that God would give them the land He had promised them was tested;

b. the people grumbled against Moses, treated the Lord with contempt, and refused to believe His promise;

c. the people sinned through unbelief;

d. God sentenced them to 40 years of wandering; none of the adults would enter Canaan;

e. the people should have learned that God always keeps His word.

5. God reminded the people, "Do not harden your hearts as you did at Meribah … [and] at Massah."

6. Because of unbelief the people did not enter either Canaan or God's eternal rest.

7. God warns us that we should not turn away from the Lord in unbelief!

8. We can help others by encouraging them in their faith on a daily basis.

9. The strength for encouragement comes from God's Word.

10. Both writers speak of "today."

11. Each participant should answer "mine."

12. We belong to one body, and each of us is part of it. None of us would want to lose a part of our body.

13. Try to involve all participants in the discussion by asking each one to describe a possible test from God (illness, for example). Help everyone see that God tests us so that we might trust Him ever more firmly.

14. We must believe the Word of the Gospel, God's good news of love in Jesus.

15. God's Word judges our eternal destiny.

16. Nothing can be hidden from God.

17. God's Word contains the valuable message of salvation through faith in Christ Jesus. Through His Word God creates and sustains our faith.

18. Ask a volunteer to read **Isaiah 53:4–6** aloud. Then ask someone else to paraphrase the good news stated there.

19. All who remain faithful until the time of death will receive this rest.

The Word for Us

Use this section to help participants apply the truth of the Word to their lives. Again, a key word is *encouragement*. As a leader, practice encouraging the participants. You will be amazed at how contagious it becomes. As you encourage, use affirmative phrases such as "very good," "thank you," "that's excellent," and "I know you can do it." God moves Christians to help one another. As leader you can set the example.

1. Answers will vary. Encourage responses such as "a new appreciation for what Jesus has done for us."

2. Don't let this turn into a gripe session about the pastor, board of elders, worship committee, etc. Insist that participants look for *helpful* ideas to improve the worship in your congregation. Appoint someone to bring these suggestions to those who plan your worship services.

3. Perhaps someone can summarize your group's suggestions and write them up for the Sunday bulletin or a congregational newsletter.

4. Encourage participants to fix their minds on the things of God—His Word, Baptism, the Lord's Supper, His forgiveness, etc.

5. Each Christian has that responsibility.

6. Some individuals are reluctant to share deeply emotional experiences. God may use that sharing, however, to strengthen and encourage others. Don't force responses, but do allow them to come. (Silence may frighten you, but allow at least 15 seconds of silence for people to build up the courage to speak!)

7. In heaven God will shield us from every trouble, but during our lives here on earth we must recognize that trouble will come to every one of us. Ask volunteers to read aloud the verses. Remind group members of the certainty that we will fail when we try to face troubles with our own strength. Encourage participants to ask God to keep them faithful during times of trouble and to use those situations to strengthen their faith.

8. God sees all. He also provides physical or spiritual healing to all who come to Him in faith.

9. We are saved only by grace through faith in Jesus as our Savior.

10. Encourage discussion in groups of three. Have each group share ways of growing in the Word of God.

Closing

Pray that, as a result of this study, God will have led you and the participants to conclude that

a. God does test His people at times in order to cause them to trust Him more and more;

b. we must hear and believe God's Word;

c. only by faith in Jesus will we enter eternal rest with God;

d. as believers in Jesus and members of His church we have a responsibility to encourage one another in our Christian faith;

e. God also calls upon us to warn one another to remain faithful to Him.

Pray together the prayer in the Study Guide. Encourage the participants to prepare for next week's lesson by reading **Hebrews 4:14–5:10** and asking for God's Spirit to guide them to a new appreciation for the everyday work of Jesus in their life.

Lesson 4
Who Needs It, Anyway? (Hebrews 4:14–5:10)

Before the Session
Read **Hebrews 4:14–5:10.** Review what you learned about high priests in lesson 2. Also read about Melchizedek in **Genesis 14:18–20.**

Getting Started
As the participants assemble, divide them into groups of three. Appoint one person in each threesome to be the intermediary; the other two people cannot speak to each other except through the intermediary. Then have those two people in each group discuss these questions through the intermediary:
- What did you pray about today? Why?
- What answers to prayer did you see today?

In this session we seek to help participants grow in their trust in Jesus as their intermediary. Encourage each person to come to the throne of God in prayer at any and every opportunity. To give class members practice in coming before the throne of God, invite them to open or close future sessions with prayer.

The Class Session
After reading the "Theme Verse" and "Goal," have one of the class members read "What's Going On Here." Ask if any have ever felt like this new Christian, hesitant to enter the chancel. It is amazing how many people in our churches are hesitant to trespass in the altar area. Set the tone for the session: It is "safe" to be close to God and the dedicated areas of the church because Jesus has paved the way for us. He is a friend!

During the Reformation God restored a great truth of the Bible to the teaching of the church. Every Christian is a member of the royal priesthood and has open access to God's throne of grace. Jesus has prepared the way for all who believe in Him to pray, to offer sacrifices, and to serve without the need of a human intercessor.

Searching the Scriptures
This is a most comforting section of Hebrews. As you work through the verses and answer the questions, point out the emphasis on Jesus Christ and His work today as He is sitting at the right hand of the Father.
1. Jesus is our great High Priest.

2. Jesus is our Mediator with the Father, inviting us to approach with confidence.

3. Faith keeps alive the relationship between us and God. Therefore, it is absolutely necessary when approaching God. You may wish to refer to **Hebrews 11:6** here.

4. Jesus is true man. He can sympathize with us **(4:15)**.

5. Though true man, Jesus is sinless.

6. Students should mention characteristics such as had no permanent home, slept when weary, wept, felt anguish of body and soul, felt tired, got thirsty, and mourned. Jesus felt all the emotions that we feel and suffered all the physical comforts and discomforts that we feel.

7. He knows just what I am like, what I feel, and is able to help me.

8. In order to be a perfect sacrifice, Jesus had to be without sin. Otherwise, one sinful human could have died for other sinful humans. That would not have satisfied the justice of God.

9. Have participants discuss this first in pairs. Christians feel comfort because they don't get punished for their sin. God also gives them strength to overcome temptations.

10. Jesus' love for us wipes away our fear. Ask volunteers to contrast our freedom to approach God freely with the fear built into the worship of false gods.

11. An Old Testament high priest
a. was a human selected from among other human beings;
b. represented the people before God to offer worship;
c. offered gifts and sacrifices for sin;
d. was able to deal gently with the ignorant and wayward;
e. had a divine appointment.

12. Christ
a. was appointed by God;
b. offered prayers and a sacrifice (Himself);
c. obeyed the Father's will;
d. represented humanity to God;
e. dealt gently with us.

13. Jesus prayed, "Father, if You are willing, take this cup from Me; yet not My will, but Yours be done" **(Luke 22:42)**.

14. Jesus did all this for us. You might emphasize the magnitude of God's love for us in Jesus when He took the weight of the sin of the whole human race upon Himself. Also, His love for each of us was so great that He would have died for any one of us if we had been the only person on earth!

15. "He became the source of eternal salvation." He is the only source.

16. No matter how we sin, we can go directly to the Father through Jesus.

17. We can be certain God will receive us in compassion with open arms, ready to give every gift we do not deserve.

The Word for Us

As participants work through this section, keep their concentration on Jesus and the enviable position each of us has toward Him. Encourage class members to see Jesus as a dear friend who is ready to hear our every prayer, sigh, and laugh. Encourage boldness.

1. First talk briefly about each picture of God. Then allow class members to express how this section of Hebrews has helped to shape the realization that our powerful and mighty God is understanding, caring, and loving.

2. Jesus said, "The Father will give you whatever you ask in My name" and "I will do whatever you ask in My name." Invite volunteers to share the confidence they receive through these words.

3. Have participants discuss this first in small groups. They may suggest that our strong bond with God is strengthened through Bible study, prayer, communicating about Jesus with fellow Christians, etc.

4. God is perfect, our friends are not. God understands our every weakness, but our friends, in their weakness, may judge us. God forgives all our sins, but friends may not forgive. Solicit other comparisons.

5. We can boldly ask for forgiveness because God knows, understands, and, for Jesus' sake, promises to pardon us. When Jesus became one with us in our human flesh, He "walked a mile in our moccasins."

6. Jesus forgives *every* sin. However, He demands that we repent and turn away from sin. Note that we in no way *earn* forgiveness through repentance. Rather, repentance is simply a condition of the human heart that believes in Jesus as our Savior and therefore abhors sin. Repentance does not cause God to forgive. God calls us by His Holy Spirit and moves us to repent so that we will receive the forgiveness He freely gives.

7. The psalmist prayed, "Forgive my hidden faults."

8. Expect responses to include thankfulness.

9. Talk about the boldness we have because Jesus walked this road for us and invites us to follow.

10. We *all* are priests who may approach the throne of God through Jesus Christ in order to intercede for others.

11. People tend to respect their pastors when they remember that the pastors are called servants of God who bring God's Word to them, counsel them with tender care, and gently guide them. Talk about ways we show

this respect.

12. Our sacrifices today include

a. ourselves as living sacrifices;

b. our gifts and offerings;

c. praise;

d. doing good and sharing with others.

13. Use the Study Guide question as a discussion starter. Allow people to share times when they felt God did or did not seem near. Encourage one another to be bold before God, knowing that in Christ we have salvation.

14. Encourage people to become more active in their lives in Christ by taking a significant step toward growing in Him.

Closing

Pray that, as a result of this study, God will have led you and the participants to conclude that

a. we no longer need earthly priests because Jesus, the eternal Son of God, became the final Word and final Priest;

b. Jesus, who took on human flesh and blood and truly understands us, deals gently with us;

c. we can boldly approach God's throne because Jesus has prepared the way for us and invites us to come to God in prayer through Himself;

d. through faith in Jesus as our Savior, God forgives every sin of commission and omission.

Remind the participants that as priests before God, they can approach Him in prayer. Ask for a volunteer to wrap up the session in prayer. If people are shy, give them practice in praying before others by using the prayer in the Study Guide. Encourage the participants to prepare for next week's lesson by reading **Hebrews 5:11–6:20.** Encourage them to remember their role as a priest before God.

Lesson 5

Getting Out of the Nursery (Hebrews 5:11–6:20)

Before the Session

Carefully read **Hebrews 5:11–6:20.** Evaluate your faith-life. Are you like the land that produces a useful crop or is your faith full of thorns and thistles? What useful crops has the Holy Spirit produced through you?

Getting Started

This could be an interesting—and maybe difficult—session to lead! People tend to resist change and often will say, "We never did it that way before" (often called the seven last words of the church). Challenge your participants to be honest with themselves and with one another and list some things in their faith and church that they don't want to see changed. (This list may include topics ranging from Communion practices to the color of the carpet in the chancel.) Now challenge them to list some things that they wouldn't mind being changed. Do any of the lists overlap? Provoke yourself and the other class members to begin the growth process. It may be painful. Growth doesn't happen without pain.

The Class Session

Ask a volunteer to read "What's Going On Here" in the Study Guide. Permit a brief discussion of the term "confirmation syndrome" and the description of it, but move rather quickly from this section into the "meat" of the lesson, the study and application of the Word. Ask God to help you and the others in your group to grow and mature as you live your lives in Christ and rely on Him completely.

Searching the Scriptures

This portion of the lesson deals with immaturity, carelessness, and doubt. As you work through these areas and seek to help members of your group to grow, encourage them often.

1. Allow participants to summarize these verses. Possible responses:

a. Stay away from evil and think as a Christian adult would think.

b. As we get into God's Word, we grow up and become stable in our Christian lives.

c. As we grow in the grace and knowledge of God, He will help us guard against evil.

Grow summarizes God's desire here.

2. Individually we are responsible for our own slow or lazy condition of contented sinfulness.

3. The people still needed to learn the elementary truths of faith.

4. We understand God's will as we carefully study His Word and digest it by the Spirit's power.

5. God gives us wisdom through His Word; it is not a by-product of age.

6. Desire for only the elementary truths, wanting to be spoon-fed by teachers, ignorance or denial of what is right or wrong, and ignorance or rejection of the new life in Jesus all contribute to delayed spiritual growth.

Other factors include a perceived lack of time, poor use of time, undisciplined use of resources, and "just getting by."

7. God encourages constant use of His Word. Through it He trains us to know good and evil and helps us overcome the latter.

8. The writer mentions the elementary foundation of "repentance" (the change of mind brought about by God's grace that results in turning away from sin and useless rituals); "faith in God" (the turning to confidence in God's grace); "instruction about baptisms" (probably the Jewish baptism of proselytes, John the Baptizer's baptism, and the baptism commanded by Jesus); "the laying on of hands" (probably in connection with ordaining, commissioning, healing, and bestowal of blessings); "the resurrection of the dead" (of all people on the Last Day); and "eternal judgment" (the destiny of those who reject God's saving grace and persist in their sinful ways). Modern-day Christians may identify memorizing the catechism and learning the liturgy as elementary aspects of their faith.

9. Only God's power can make us grow spiritually. He manifests His power through the means of grace (Word and Sacrament).

10. Paul instructed Timothy to remind others of what the Lord says: avoid quarreling, learn and study God's truth, avoid gossip and false teachings, trust the Lord, confess His name.

11. Rejection of Christ will cause one to miss out on the resurrection to life in heaven.

12. The sin against the Holy Spirit—a hardening of the heart. By rejecting God's Spirit and His teaching, those who once knew Him as Savior and Lord disgrace Him. Repentance is possible only in connection with faith, but the very nature of the sin against the Holy Spirit is to cut oneself off from God's efforts to create faith. Assure participants that those who fear they have committed that sin show by that very fear that they have not committed it. Therefore the door to repentance and forgiveness remains open.

13. Paul reminds us to beware of becoming filled with pride and believing we have it made. As we get more deeply into God's Word, He keeps us firmly grounded. God's Word is a means of grace, a way by which we receive His grace.

14. We become productive by continuing to be attached to Jesus and drawing strength from Him.

15. An unproductive Christian risks the danger of being cursed—now and forever.

16. Good works accompany faith. We are able to do them because God has made us alive in Christ. Through them God is glorified and people are turned toward Him.

17. The people stood strong in suffering and under ridicule and insult. They also encouraged others who were suffering and in prison. They willingly sacrificed material possessions.

18. We are assured that God will not forget us or our work. We are to build up our hope by showing "diligence" in the things of God.

19. Paul points out that God can use suffering as part of the growth process. Through it He makes our hope secure so we may live unafraid.

20. God encourages us to imitate examples of faith and patience, both gifts from God.

21. Abraham was willing to sacrifice his only son, but God provided a ram instead, thereby also foreshadowing the sacrifice of His only Son as our Substitute.

22. God swore the oath by Himself. (One can only swear by one greater than oneself. There is none greater than God, so He swore by His own name.) God cannot and does not lie.

23. Trust in God's promises increases our hope in Him.

24. By God's grace we know that we, too, will enter that "inner sanctuary"—heaven itself.

25. Through Baptism into Christ, we take part in His resurrection.

The Word for Us

Discussion here should help all the participants see ways they can improve their attitude and increase their desire to grow in the Lord.

1–2. Suggest working in small groups where participants may be more willing to discuss and share their own thoughts, attitudes, and suggestions. Answers will vary. These questions are intended for discussion.

3. Again, answers will vary. You should see a marked difference between the immature and the maturing. (Note: Becoming mature is a process. On earth there is no such thing as a matured Christian who no longer needs to grow spiritually.)

4. Growth happens as a result of "constant use" of God's Word and a willingness on our part to grow beyond the elementary stages of faith.

5. Do not insist that participants share, but do provide that opportunity for volunteers.

6. Many rites and traditions, like confirmation, are connected only to the elementary truths of God's Word. By stopping with the rite, and not growing beyond it, spiritual growth is arrested.

7. God warns us to look out; we may go backwards and fall from the faith. Yet we can assure everyone that in Christ *all* sins are forgiven.

8. Only through God's Spirit do we grow up in Christ. The Spirit always works with the Word of God.

9. Seek answers like "getting into the Word," "applying the Word to my life," "paying attention in church," "frequent attendance at Communion."
10. We have the assurance that God "will not forget."
11. Encourage members to offer suggestions.
12. We know God's Word is always true and trustworthy. God will keep His promises.
13. Don't force individuals to respond, but be sure to allow time for hesitant participants to speak.
14. Allow participants to spend a few minutes on this. Encourage them to trust the Lord, who will never leave us or forsake us.

Closing

Pray that, as a result of this study, God will have led you and the participants to conclude that

a. God desires more than simple knowledge, traditions, and rites;

b. God provides us with spiritual growth as we dig deeply into His Word;

c. God calls Christians to be productive—producing fruit for God through their life in His kingdom;

d. God, who will take His own to be with Him forever, is completely trustworthy and His Word is sure.

Ask for a volunteer to close in prayer, perhaps using the prayer in the lesson. Encourage class members to try to put some of the truths of this lesson to work this week by digging deeply into **Hebrews 7.** It has a lot of meat, so they should read it carefully.

Lesson 6

The Great Melchizedek (Hebrews 7)

Before the Session

Read **Hebrews 7.** Also review what you learned about Melchizedek in lesson 4 and in **Genesis 14:18–20.**

Getting Started

Gather the group together for a comparative discussion of religions. As people name religions, write the name on the board or on a piece of chart paper. Then go back and list under each religion its requirements for believers. You will soon notice that only the Christian religion has no requirements—Jesus Christ alone is the Way, the Truth, and the Life. As you lead your group through the study of the Word, emphasize Christ's superiority. Then apply this truth to the lives of all participants. God be with you as you lead this most important lesson.

The Class Session

Ask a volunteer to read "What's Going On Here." In this session you begin to dig more deeply into the Word. Encourage each participant to do just that—to dig deeply and to grow up in the Lord.

Searching the Scriptures

As participants seek to learn about Melchizedek, avoid getting bogged down in details. Constantly point to him as a type of Christ. Then focus on Christ, the eternal Son of God, the one perfect High Priest, whose sacrifice has everlasting value.

1. Qualities of Melchizedek:

a. King of righteousness

b. King of peace

c. Without father or mother (Melchizedek was a human being like us, but the writer notes that, unlike other important figures in the Old Testament, Melchizedek's family history [c, d, e] is not given in order to portray him as a prefiguration of Christ)

d. Without genealogy

e. Without beginning or end of life

f. Like the Son of God

g. Perpetual (as with c, d, and e, this characteristic prefigures the new High Priest, Jesus—**Psalm 110:4**).

2. Qualities of Levitical priests:

a. Selected from among men

b. Appointed by law

c. Represented the people in offering sacrifices

d. Weak

e. Descendant of Levi (answer inferred)

f. Temporary

3. Qualities of Jesus, the great High Priest:

a. From the tribe of Judah (no earthly priest ever came from that tribe)

b. Became a priest by an oath of God (see **Psalm 110:4**)

c. Able to save

d. Holy, blameless, pure, set apart from sinners, exalted above all

e. Permanent

4. Melchizedek was greater than Abraham, the father of the Israelite nation—and therefore also superior to Levitical priests, because
a. he received the tithe from Abraham;
b. he blessed Abraham.
5. Christ is superior to both Levi and Melchizedek because
a. He is sinless;
b. He offered one sacrifice for all people;
c. He is the perfect Son of God forever.
6. An earthly priest lacks both perfection and permanence. Christ offered the supreme sacrifice for us and He is perfect forever.
7. Christ became our Priest with an oath from God (God cannot lie—**Hebrews 6:18**) and has sealed the covenant by the one perfect sacrifice.
8. Jesus, who lives forever, has a permanent priesthood.
9. Christ acts as our "defense attorney" and our "dispensary." Whatever we ask through Christ, we will receive. Therefore we pray in His name and on account of His sacrifice for us.
10. God assures us, "He sacrificed for their sins once for all when He offered Himself."
11. Ask someone to read the references aloud. If everyone has the same translation of the Bible, you might have the group read **1 Corinthians 15:54–57** in unison. These would be good words to memorize so participants can share them with someone whose Christian loved one has died. We attain an indestructible life when we are joined by faith to our indestructible Savior.
12. God has provided only one Advocate—Jesus. He meets our needs and is able to take all our requests before God.

The Word for Us

Questions in this section have been designed to help participants appreciate anew the fact that they can do nothing to earn God's favor and that they really can trust Jesus, and Him alone. Be sure to encourage this trust.
1. Those who do not believe in Jesus will not enter heaven.
2. Jesus is the only one who can take our sins away.
3. Jesus assures us, "I and the Father are one." The Father is God, so Jesus is also God.
4. God uses the knowledge of Jesus to point us to the reality of the truth of His Word and so keeps us from any false trust or false hope. Since none of us is perfect, it is a false hope to trust in our own goodness.
5. On our own we can never please God. We need a "go-between." When we forget that, we begin to trust in ourselves or others who are unable to assist us. God uses His Word (verses like **Hebrews 7:26–28**) to increase

our trust.

6. Because other trust depends on the Law, it is weak, useless, and unable to draw us to God.

7. Our biggest need is for forgiveness. As true God, Jesus can help us. He and the Father are able to supply our every need.

8. The writer emphasizes the perfection of Jesus and His complete sacrifice for our sins.

9. Jesus lives to intercede for us.

10. Because Jesus died and lives for us, we receive forgiveness of all our sins.

11. Have participants discuss this question in groups of two or three. Then encourage a few volunteers to share responses with the entire group.

Closing

Pray that, as a result of this study, God will have led you and the participants to conclude that

a. we have only one Savior, Jesus;

b. no human religion or system is capable of bringing us to God;

c. no matter how good we might be, only our righteousness because of Christ makes us acceptable to God;

d. Jesus loves to answer our prayers;

e. only Jesus can bring our prayers to the Father.

Assure the group that God truly loves every one of them and in Jesus will answer our every prayer. Remind them that God blesses us not only when we hear the Word, but also when we do what it says. Then pray together (or have a volunteer pray) the prayer in the Study Guide. Have them read **Hebrews 8** and look through the questions of the next lesson to prepare for your next classtime.

Lesson 7

God's New Arrangement (Hebrews 8)

Before the Session

Read **Hebrews 8** carefully. Then review the three major types of covenants referred to in Scripture: the Royal Grant, or unconditional covenant, whereby a king grants an unconditional gift to his servant (no reciprocal action by the servant is required); Parity Covenant, a covenant between equals, with equal actions by both parties; Suzerain-vassal Covenant, a conditional agreement between a king and his vassals, whereby the king pledged protection in exchange for the loyalty and service of his servants.

Getting Started

You have the privilege of leading this session on the two covenants God made with His people, those of old and those of the present. What a joy it is to live in the new covenant with our blessed Savior! Jesus has fulfilled all the requirements of the Law for us and has by His own blood paid the price of our sins.

As the class gathers together, continue to compare the old covenant with the new covenant, drawing on what has been learned in previous sessions. Encourage participants to think about some ways in which they can serve the Lord out of love, not out of fear.

The Class Session

Ask a volunteer to read aloud "What's Going On Here." (Or have each read it silently.) Then pose a question such as, "What would you think if some Sunday morning as you entered your church there was a blazing fire at the altar and a priest was offering God a lamb as a burnt offering for your sins? How do you think you would react?" Allow the class to think and talk about it for a few moments. Then go on to "Searching the Scriptures," which should lead all to a greater appreciation of the new arrangement God has made for us.

Searching the Scriptures

As you begin your study of the Word in **Hebrews 8,** note the emphasis on how God deals with our sins. There is a contrast between the old and the new covenants as well as the assurance that God has handled all our sins in Jesus and has set us free to live for Him.

1. We have sinned and fall short of God's glory.
2. Through one man—Jesus—God has taken away the punishment of sin and has overcome death.
3. The old covenant required daily sacrifices. Through them God assured the people that He, who had delivered them from Egypt, was dwelling among them.
4. Christ sacrificed Himself only once, because He made all believers holy through that one perfect sacrifice.
5. Christ offered His own blood.

6. Through Christ we receive cleansing from our sins.

7. The sacrifices, which were a reminder of sins and pointed to Christ, were in themselves inadequate because animal blood cannot take away human sin.

8. God told Moses to build the tabernacle exactly according to directions. It is a copy of the heavenly tabernacle.

9. The people, with their willful sinning, caused the old covenant to need replacement.

10. The people were not faithful to God and His covenant.

11. God said, "This is the covenant *I will make.*"

12. God says, "I will make [a covenant] … put My laws in their minds and write them on their hearts … be their God … forgive their wickedness … remember their sins no more."

13. God's grace costs us nothing.

14. God promises to forget our sins.

15. Answers should surely include the peace that comes from knowing we are completely forgiven.

16. God said, "I will be their God, and they will be My people."

17. God said, "I will put My laws in their minds and write them on their hearts."

18. Paul writes that the regulations of the Law "lack any value in restraining sensual indulgence."

19. Paul encourages us to set our minds on heavenly things (God's will). We can do this because Christ gives us His new life and power. God also promises that we will appear in the glory of heaven with Jesus.

The Word for Us

Questions in this section are designed to help people express how they might serve the Lord and their neighbor in love.

1. You might have participants first discuss this in small groups. Because Christ is eternal, we have a solid base for our hope.

2. Since Christ serves in the tabernacle of heaven, which has been set up by God and which is "the real thing," we know He is eternal.

3. After small-group discussion, look for an emphasis on the reality of the grace of God as revealed to us in the new covenant.

4. Encourage participants to share ways these "things" help them worship. Remember that objects are mere shadows; they provide real help only when they point beyond themselves—to God.

5. Just like the objects used in worship in the old covenant, ours, too, will pass. Also, their value lies not in themselves but in the way they point us to God.

6. The new covenant points us to the peace that comes through forgiveness because of Christ.

7. God has completely dealt with sin once and for all in Jesus. He paid for our sin and received our punishment.

8. God's grace assures us that because Jesus met the measure of perfection for us, we always have a place in His family. This does not depend on us, but on God.

9. Through the blood of Jesus, God does not even remember our sins. (Don't expect to understand this. Rather, trust this fact from God's Word.)

10. Because God has forgiven us, we will forgive others and will not require acts of penance from them. We can do this because God has made us "alive with Christ" **(Ephesians 2:4–5, 10).** See also **2 Corinthians 5:15.**

11. Discuss in small groups. If some participants wish to share with the large group, permit them to do so.

12. List responses on a chalkboard or chart. Encourage commitments to one or more items.

13. Lead participants to conclude that God works through the means of grace. Thus, as we feed on Word and Sacrament, He strengthens our faith.

14. God's laws and will are now written in our heart. God's Spirit gives the strength to do the will of God.

15. Ask two or three volunteers to share their perceptions of how God's grace empowers us.

16. Allow about one minute for everyone to write a response. Do not ask them to share orally.

Closing

Pray that, as a result of this study, God will have led you and the participants to conclude that

a. when Christ suffered, died, and rose from death and subsequently ascended into heaven, He sealed a new covenant that is quite unlike the old;

b. God no longer requires the sacrifice of burnt offerings to atone for sin (the blood of animals can never overcome sin);

c. because no one can keep the Law of God perfectly, Christ came to be our perfect High Priest to keep the Law in our place;

d. God forgives sins simply and wholly on the basis of Christ's sacrifice for us;

e. by faith in Christ we have forgiveness of all sin and guilt and can now live to please God and our neighbor.

Have someone read the prayer in the Study Guide. Encourage class members to prepare for the next session by thinking of "one of a kind" items and by reading **Hebrews 9:1–10:18.**

Lesson 8
Once for All ... (Hebrews 9:1–10:18)

Before the Session
Read **Hebrews 9:1–10:18.** Think about different ways you might serve God. Remember that service to God is nothing more or less than acts of thanksgiving to God, who through Jesus has paid for our sins "once for all." You may want to do some research on **Exodus 25–31** and **35–40** in order to be more prepared to lead this session.

Getting Started
Make **Hebrews 9:14** a special verse for you and your group. It emphasizes that we have been cleansed so that we might serve the living God. Read through it together, then challenge class participants to write out plans of how they can give thanks to God through service to other people. Use your discretion as to whether or not to have participants share their plans with the class.

The Class Session
Ask a volunteer to read "What's Going On Here" from the Study Guide. The historical material is intended to help the students to see that in many ways we mimic the Old Testament people in our ways of worship. It is also intended to set the stage for understanding that there is nothing we can do to add to what has already been done for us by Christ.

Searching the Scriptures
Some of these questions get at tough theological issues. Help the class to dig into Scripture for the answers. Provide those answers for them only as a last resort.

1. Anything portable is only temporary and will pass away. Only that which is heavenly will remain.

2. The words "the way into the Most Holy Place had not yet been disclosed as long as the first tabernacle was still standing" indicate that as soon as the Christ came, the old would be abolished.

3. The sacrifices "were not able to clear the conscience"; they could not forgive sin.

4. The "external regulations" were in effect only "until the time of the new order," the new covenant.

5. The perfect tabernacle "is not man-made … not a part of this creation," that is, it is not tainted by the sinfulness of humans but is rather made by the perfect God.

6. Life is found in the blood. Blood makes atonement.

7. "Without the shedding of blood there is no forgiveness" **(Hebrews 9:22).**

8. Sin has broken our relationship with God. It is like a wall that we cannot penetrate.

9. The shedding of blood is necessary for forgiveness.

10. Blood was required because death was a necessary part of the covenant—death of animals under the old covenant and death of the Lamb of God under the new.

11. Jesus, the perfect sacrifice (Lamb), shed His blood to cleanse us from all sin.

12. Our acts lead to death; the unblemished sacrifice of Christ cleanses us. We are cleansed "so that we may serve the living God."

13. We are purified by a better sacrifice—the blood of Jesus.

14. Christ entered the Most Holy Place only once.

15. Christ will appear a second time to take believers to eternal glory.

16. We have been made holy by Jesus' sacrifice.

17. Sin, the devil, and the last enemy—death—become Christ's footstool.

18. God assures us, " 'Their sins and lawless acts I will remember no more' … there is no longer any sacrifice for sin." He forgives completely.

The Word for Us

If participants have examined this session in advance, invite them to tell which questions they would especially like to discuss. Spend most of your time with those questions. Some questions have no "right" or "wrong" answers; use the discussion to personalize the miracle of God's love in the sacrifice of Jesus.

1. Our acts cannot clear our conscience.

2. Christ's sacrifice has indeed atoned for the sin and guilt our conscience brings before us.

3. We demonstrate our forgiveness by serving God in word and deed.

4. Probably most of us try to win God's approval through acts of love, of worship, of giving, etc. God clearly teaches that *all* these attempts fail because of our sinful condition. It is only through the shedding of blood that we can receive forgiveness.

5. We can *look forward to* Christ's Second Coming because we know He will take us to eternal glory. Unbelievers, however, *should* fear the judgment.

6. Have participants work in pairs to select a verse of assurance, such as **Hebrews 10:17.**

7. It is impossible for obedience to take away sin because we cannot even begin to keep the Law perfectly, nor can we overcome sin by any other work. We become acceptable to God only through the shedding of Christ's blood.

8. We have been set apart by God to serve Him with our whole being.

9. Discuss this in small groups first. Look for responses that tell how rituals and forms point us to Christ—the source of power for our lives.

10. Again, discuss in small groups first. Then ask several groups to share their conclusions.

11. Begin with small-group discussion here, too. Responses should include thankfulness for the forgiveness of Christ and the love of God that fills our hearts through the power of the Holy Spirit.

12. Give individuals time to page through a hymnal. Some might suggest lines from "Just as I Am, Without One Plea"; "Amazing Grace, How Sweet the Sound"; "Salvation unto Us Has Come"; "Jesus, Your Blood and Righteousness."

13. Allow time for participants to carry out this activity. Encourage them to memorize the verse.

Closing

Pray that, as a result of this study, God will have led you and the participants to conclude that

a. our life with God depends on the gift of forgiveness bought by Christ;

b. since there is no forgiveness without the shedding of blood, it is impossible to win favor or forgiveness by our own acts or deeds;

c. we can be absolutely sure of forgiveness through Jesus Christ, who will come on the Last Day to take His own to glory;

d. we have been cleansed from our sins so that we might serve God out of thankfulness for the gift of forgiveness.

Then ask a volunteer to pray the prayer in the Study Guide or to offer a prayer from the heart. Encourage preparation for next week's lesson. It will help to prepare us for the rest of our lives.

Lesson 9
Hang in There (Hebrews 10:19–39)

Before the Session
As you plan for this session, read **Hebrews 10:39.** Get ready to talk about how you will be prepared to endure hardships that may come into your life.

Getting Started
After participants have gathered, point out that this lesson highlights three main themes. The first theme deals with growing in confidence in the Lord Jesus and encouraging one another. Some of that encouragement has to do with worship, and some of it has to do with fellowship and doing good works for the glory of God. Always, the highest purpose for these works is to give God glory.

A second theme has to do with willful or deliberate sin. Encourage participants to recognize any such sins they may have fallen into, repent of them, and resolve not to sin in the same manner.

The third theme is centered on enduring, even when it is most difficult. The overall theme is "hang in there." At the end, you will have life forever with the one in whom you have placed your confidence—Jesus!

The Class Session
Have a participant who can read with emphasis read aloud "What's Going On Here." If possible, choose a person who is having a difficult time in life and can truly identify with the theme of the lesson. Since Christ is the very center of the lesson and is central in the book of Hebrews, especially point out that only He can give the strength to "hang in there." Allow time for brief comments and discussion before continuing.

Searching the Scriptures
As noted above, this lesson contains three distinct themes. In this section they are somewhat intertwined and yet remain distinct.

1. Because of Jesus' high priestly sacrifice we are able to "draw near to God" **(Hebrews 10:22)**, "hold unswervingly to the hope we profess" **(verse 23)**, and "spur one another on" **(verse 24).**

2. By the blood of Jesus, who has opened the way into the sanctuary of heaven, we may approach God with total confidence.

3. We have been clothed with Christ in Baptism.

4. Christ has made us clean by the washing of Baptism.

5. The blood of Jesus has cleansed us, has given us "a sincere heart" that trusts God unhesitatingly.

6. God is faithful to the very end.

7. The exhortations of other Christians spur us on.

8. We do not know when the Last Day will come, but as each day passes, that Day of the Lord draws closer.

9. The words "We have received the knowledge of the truth" indicate that God is speaking to believers.

10. God threatens judgment and hell, with no opportunity to repent.

11. When we deliberately continue to sin, we are trampling Christ underfoot and treating His holy blood and covenant with disdain. We are also insulting the Spirit's gifts of graces and life in Christ.

12. God is just and will avenge Himself.

13. Paul warns us to stay away from every evil, especially the temptations offered by unbelievers.

14. Be sure, as you review the sin against the Holy Spirit, to point out again the certainty of God's salvation. God's threat is very real. (Deliberately and persistently to shut out the Holy Spirit makes it impossible for us to be forgiven, for without His work in our lives it is impossible to repent or come to faith.) But God's comfort is also very real, for the Holy Spirit is active in us when we feel concern about having committed the sin against the Holy Spirit. Therefore we can be positive that we do receive God's forgiveness for the sake of Christ.

15. Invite participants to share times when they have seen other Christians exhibit qualities similar to those of the Hebrew Christians who stood their ground in the face of suffering; were publicly exposed to insult and persecution; stood side by side with those who were persecuted; sympathized with those in prison; joyfully accepted the confiscation of their property.

16. The people knew they had a better life and "better and lasting possessions."

17. God-given confidence grasps God's blessings in this life and ultimately in heaven.

18. If everyone has the same Bible translation, read **verse 39** in unison.

The Word for Us

Encourage discussion as you work through this section. Also encourage participants to share their findings and even some intimate parts of their lives with a friend or a fellow class member. (Most will probably feel comfortable sharing by this time in the course.)

1. First discuss in groups of two, three, or four. Then ask several volunteers to share their responses with the large group. God invites us to worship without fear in the confidence we receive through our faith in Jesus and through our Baptism.

2. Again, begin with small groups. Answers will vary.

3. Use small groups again. Some may even mention that they ask others to give them encouragement. Finally, God through His Word gives us the power to overcome.

4. Repeat the small-group procedure. Christian maturity, God empowers us to receive exhortation as coming from one who loves and cares about us.

5. Encourage very specific responses, possibly varying according to the person and the situation.

6. One response would be to remember whose we are and whom we serve.

7. Only the Holy Spirit can stop the drifting.

8. Continued willful sinning leads to judgment from God.

9. Discuss the activity together. If necessary, point out that there is a difference between being enmeshed in a bad habit (and struggling against it) and adopting an "I don't care" attitude. Encourage participants (silently and personally) to identify the friend they may select as they commit themselves to this activity.

10. Possible answers:

Determination: sticking with it

Responsibility: being trustworthy

Patience: willing to wait it out

Diligence: continuing to work hard

Self-control: maintaining calm in midst of storm

11. A solid foundation begins with a firm trust in the promises of a faithful God and is secure in that trust.

12. Discuss first in small groups. Answers should recognize that power *from God* enables us to stand firm.

13. Build on the discussion from the previous question. Often God provides His power differently for different people and different situations.

14. We need to recognize that "why?" is usually the wrong question to ask. **Hebrews 10:32–39** shows us how Christians throughout the ages have suffered and how God has stayed with them, enabling them to endure their trials. So we, too, are encouraged to use the power God provides.

15. By God's gift of faith we hold to Jesus and are righteous in Him and certain of the power He provides.

16. Encourage small groups to respond to one another.

17. Encourage this exercise. Use **Hebrews 10:23–24** as an alternate.

Closing

Pray that, as a result of this study, God will have led you and the participants to conclude that

a. we can approach God in our private and public worship, confident that we are accepted by Him;

b. God wants us to encourage one another so that together we will worship and live out our lives to glorify Him;

c. continued, willful sin can and will lead to separation from God;

d. even though we can expect trials of faith, through Christ God will empower us to endure and to encourage others to endure as they "hang in there."

Keep these in mind as you ask a volunteer to lead the group in prayer, using the prayer in the Study Guide, if desired. Encourage participants to read all of **Hebrews 11** carefully to prepare for the next session, when you will talk about those examples of strong faith who have gone before. As a brief homework assignment, have participants complete question 9 of "Searching the Scriptures" before the next class session.

Lesson 10

The Hall of Faith (Hebrews 11)

Before the Session

Prepare for this session by reading carefully **Hebrews 11.** With which of these members of the Hall of Faith do you most closely identify? Why? Keep this in mind as you lead others to study this chapter.

Getting Started

As participants arrive, have them informally share with one another who their heroes of faith are and why. These heroes may be from the Bible, from history, or from their own lives. Be aware that comparing one's faith with that of others can sometimes lead to low self-esteem and feelings of worthlessness. To thwart this, remind participants that each person who has faith in Jesus will be inducted into the "Hall of Faith" with all believers on the Last Day (see **Hebrews 11:40**). Thus no believer is better than another in the sight of God.

Also help participants recognize that as we put our faith into action we grow and are numbered with the "greats."

The Class Session

Ask a good reader to read "What's Going On Here." It stresses that faith is a gift God grants to every believer. God also empowers us to put our faith into action. If questions arise, take time to answer briefly as best you can or make sure the question will be addressed later in the session. Then move quickly to "Searching the Scriptures."

Searching the Scriptures

As participants work through the initial questions, they should be developing insights that will help them write their own definition of *faith* (question 7). Question 8 has many parts; try to move quickly through this material. Ask volunteers to complete question 9 at home, either before or after the session.

1. Faith is confidence. It looks in hope to the future. It has as its object things that are not seen.

2. Faith is necessary in order to please God. It believes that God is real. It believes that He rewards those who seek Him.

3. At the Last Day Christians will receive "something better." Now we hope for that which is not yet realized.

4. The Old Testament heroes of faith did not live to see the coming of the Messiah. Belief and hope are necessary components of faith.

5. Although we do not see heaven now, we know God has promised heaven and will fulfill His promise. Heaven is very real in our lives. **2 Corinthians 5:7** puts faith and sight in opposition to each other.

6. God created everything by His command.

7. Allow a couple minutes for each participant to write his or her own definition. It should reflect the truths of the previous questions.

8. **Hebrews 11** says the following:

a. Abel presented his offering in faith. By faith he was righteous and still speaks.

b. Enoch pleased God by faith. He was taken bodily to heaven.

c. Noah built the ark. By faith he condemned the world for its sinfulness and became an heir of righteousness.

d. Abraham obeyed God's call. He formed a new nation.

—Abraham lived as an alien. He looked to the sure hope of the eternal, not to the present.

—Abraham became the father of Isaac. He had many descendants by Isaac.

—Abraham offered Isaac. He received Isaac back as one risen from the dead.

e. Isaac blessed Jacob and Esau. The future of the messianic line was assured.

f. Jacob blessed the sons of Joseph and so assured the future.

g. Joseph encouraged the exodus and asked to be buried in the Promised Land, thus setting the stage for future events.

h. Moses' parents had the faith and courage to defy Pharaoh's decree that all Hebrew baby boys should die. Thus Moses, who would someday lead God's people to the Promised Land, was kept alive.

i. Moses chose disgrace for the sake of Christ. He looked to the future.

—Moses led the people out of Egypt. God's people were able to leave slavery.

—Moses kept the Passover. The firstborn were spared.

j. Rahab concealed the spies. Her life was spared and she became an ancestor of Jesus.

k. Gideon and the others were, in summary, active in faith, not passive. God's kingdom was preserved and grew.

9. Allow several minutes for participants to share their findings (completed at home).

10. Ask someone to read **Hebrews 11:33–34** aloud. Then ask the group to apply the words to today's Christians. The persecution today's Christians face may be more subtle than these biblical examples, but strong faith in the Lord will help us persevere and be strong witnesses.

11. Again, ask someone to read the verses aloud. Discuss troubles and difficulties we can expect today. Emphasize that we do not go out looking for trouble, but if it comes, God helps us endure.

12. The resurrection to eternal life on the Last Day—far better than release from torture at the cost of denying their faith.

13. The saints don't "shrink back," but remain confident.

14. The word *all* encourages each of us.

15. Encourage each participant to memorize several verses.

The Word for Us

1. Invite volunteers to identify a "faith-filled" person and to tell why they selected this person. You might first do this in small groups.

2. Don't ask for oral responses. Do allow time to write a prayer.

3. Encourage volunteers to share. Look for examples of children who demonstrate a trust that God will do as He promised.

4. Allow participants to share, first in small groups and then with the larger group.

5. God encourages us, as He did them, to put our faith into action and to move out of the realm of talk into the arena of action.

6. They and we look forward to our heavenly home.

7. Don't force anyone to respond. Probably participants will be more willing to share if they begin in small groups.

8. Discuss ways Satan uses the world around us to make us afraid that God won't come through for us. Most advertising, for example, encourages us to think about what we can do for ourselves.

9. God tests even those weak in faith in order to strengthen that faith.

10. Allow time for silent reflection. Permit oral responses but do not ask for them.

11. Discuss in small groups, and then in the larger group. God provides strength through the means of grace—His Word and sacraments.

12. When things look impossible, God is still in control and will perform His miracles (which we don't always recognize, because they may not seem spectacular to us).

13. God's ways and our ways are often different (see **Isaiah 55:9**).

14. Ask someone to read **Hebrews 11:39–40.** Then talk about the encouragement found there.

15. Discuss in small groups first. Pray that God will move both us and our friend to trust Him in all circumstances.

16. God would have us believe firmly without ever seeing what we hope for. Look again at the encouragement God provides through people like Noah, Abraham, and others. Have participants tell how they have seen similar action by God in themselves or others.

17. God will take us to heaven, where we will rejoice, give thanks, praise, etc.

Closing

Pray that, as a result of this study, God will have led you and the participants to conclude that

a. faith involves confidence that God is doing and will continue to do for us what He has promised;

b. we will want to continue to live that faith;

c. faith takes God at His Word and responds to that Word without seeing the end of what has been promised;

d. God provides an attitude that will enable us boldly to step out in faith in Him and for Him and His kingdom.

Wrap up this session with prayer. Ask to a volunteer to pray, either from the heart or the one printed in the Study Guide. As participants prepare for the next session, challenge them to think about how they will remain calm in spite of whatever comes to them. They should read **Hebrews 12** in preparation for the "calm after the storm."

Lesson 11
Calm after the Storm (Hebrews 12)

Before the Session

Carefully read **Hebrews 12** to prepare for today's lesson. As you read, think about the times and ways that you have felt God's discipline. How did He sustain you? What were the benefits of the discipline?

The Christian life is indeed a disciplined life! As a leader of this study, you know the discipline needed to prepare for and lead each lesson. In this lesson you will be learning, along with the class, the Lord's discipline and the self-discipline necessary to run the race that has been set before us.

Getting Started

As class members gather, talk about what sort of training is required for an athlete to get into shape for a race. If your class includes athletes, have them share the steps of their training regime. Then help participants speak more freely about "getting in shape" to run the race of life and to be ready and willing to help one another. Your words of encouragement, your actions, your own self-discipline, and especially your attitude as you lead this session will speak loudly and clearly to the class. People often open up if they are given the freedom to speak personally without fear of losing their self-esteem. You can help them by accepting them, just as they are. Above all, assure them that, because they are members of God's church, they are forgiven and their names are written in heaven.

Then discuss the theme of the lesson: "Calm after the Storm." Life is filled with many different storms as we run the race laid out by God. At the end there is a peaceful kingdom prepared for us from the foundation of the world. Emphasize that the forgiveness of Christ brings us that calm every day and that His blood brings the eternal calm.

The Class Session

Have a volunteer read "What's Going on Here" in the Study Guide. Some in your group may wish to talk about an athletic event recently observed, some of their own contests, or the training and competition one of their children has experienced. Allow a few minutes for this, since it will assist with the rest of the lesson. Others may speak to the word *discipline*. Again, allow some discussion, but move on quickly, because that will be covered rather thoroughly in the study. You may break in on the "rambling" of the group by saying something like, "Let's see what this chapter says about that." Then go quickly into "Searching the Scriptures."

Searching the Scriptures
The Arena (12:1–3)
1. Allow a short time for speculation. Some things that hinder our faith may include family ties, pleasures, "necessary" appointments, excuses, etc.
2. Entangling sins could be a wide variety of "thoughts, words, and deeds" that are contrary to God's will.
3. Jesus, who laid out the race, urges us to run with patience, perseverance, and endurance.
4. We prepare through "strict training" and by making the body a "slave" to the will.
5. We must compete according to the rules.
6. When we look to Jesus and focus our thoughts on Him, we remember the salvation He earned for us and the heavenly calling He extends to us. When our eyes are fixed on Jesus, we cannot see all the distractions of this sinful world.
7. Jesus endured the cross (suffered death), scorned its shame (overcame death), and sat down at the right hand of the Father (reigns over life and death).
8. Jesus could look forward to accomplishing our eternal redemption and being glorified at the Father's right hand.
9. Jesus helps us endure this life so we "will not grow weary and lose heart."
The Discipline (12:4–13)
1. No matter how extravagant the love, unless discipline accompanies it, there is no training for endurance under hardship; yet discipline without love is punishment that is resented.
2. These verses speak of the persecution as "the Lord's discipline."
3. Some don't take God's discipline seriously, while others cave in to discouragement from it. Each reaction fails to recognize the communication we are receiving from God.
4. The verse tells us that "the Lord disciplines those He loves." Discipline assures us that we belong to God.
5. Those not disciplined are illegitimate—not true sons—and therefore not Christians.
6. God disciplines us for our spiritual good—so that we will become stronger in faith and more productive in our Christian life.
7. We are healed by the grace of God in Jesus Christ.
Living under Grace (12:14–29)

1. Remembering that we, too, have our faults and that Jesus died for us all, we will, by the power of His Spirit, make every effort to live in harmony with others.

2. Each Christian has a responsibility to work toward harmony. When we work toward harmony, we are given the title of children of God.

3. Grace is a free gift from God that demands nothing. We dare not demand what God's grace has not required. God's free grace in our hearts empowers us to be graceful.

4. Bitterness causes trouble between people and leads them away from pure living before the Lord.

5. God warns us to resist becoming sexually immoral or permissive, using the strength we receive from Jesus, the spotless Lamb of God, who gave us the glorious promise of **Matthew 5:8.**

6. A moment of selfish pleasure can bring consequences that last throughout our lives.

7. We "have *not* come to a mountain … that is burning with fire." Our High Priest, Jesus, offers us something better.

8. Sinai symbolizes living under the Law, and Zion symbolizes living under grace. Bask in the joy God gives us by His grace.

9. This verse assures us that "we are receiving a kingdom that cannot be shaken," where all will be at peace.

The Word for Us

Many of these questions are designed to promote class discussion. Expect participants to take the Word home with them more readily when they can apply it to their lives and can have others affirm that the Word is indeed applicable to everyday living.

1. Ask for examples of friendships, etc., that take our attention away from our primary purpose in life—to live for Jesus.

2. Discuss in small groups. Then share a few responses with the larger group. Be sure someone mentions that the ultimate confidence comes from God through the means of grace, and that God uses us to encourage one another.

3. Through Word and Sacrament we keep our minds directed to that which is utterly important, which then will frame our attitude.

4. Through knowledge of their endurance God strengthens our faith and encourages us to "run with perseverance."

5. Ask each small group to agree on one way and to share it with the larger group. Above all, we encourage one another through the Gospel.

6. Share in small groups only.

7. Again, share in small groups only.

8. Someone might quote **Hebrews 12:11–13** to illustrate that God causes good (a stronger faith) to come out of suffering.

9. Begin again with small-group discussion. As in question 5, we need to share the Gospel (the power from God) as we provide *any* kind of help.

10. Practicing discipline and training and using the power provided by God in His Word enables these people to remain strong and vibrant.

11. Discipline comes from a loving God for our own good.

12. Emphasize again that only the power *God* provides can bring success to our efforts to live in peace and harmony through repentance and forgiveness.

13. The Holy Spirit, pointing us to Jesus, empowers us to repent and to live at peace.

14. Small groups might suggest various strategies they employ, always used in connection with Word and Sacrament.

15. God has already laid out the path to eternal life. When we make our own rules, we try to follow a different path and to earn that which is already ours—free of charge! When we succeed in keeping such outward rules, we may become smug, like the Pharisees. Also, such rules tend to militate against our Christian freedom.

Closing

Pray that, as a result of this study, God will have led you and the participants to conclude that

a. as we continue in training in our Christian lives, God empowers us to endure to the end;

b. God desires that we "trim down" by living in moderation and avoiding all evil;

c. God loves His children so much that He disciplines them so they will be able to endure all things for His sake;

d. God has called upon us to live by grace alone and to live in peace with our fellow Christians as we await the Last Day, when He will give the final calm.

Read together or have a volunteer read the prayer in the Study Guide.

Have participants get ready for the next session by reading and taking to heart **Hebrews 13.** Alert them to look for some directions for living in these last days.

Lesson 12
Remembering Whose You Are (Hebrews 13)

Before the Session

This last chapter appears almost as an addendum to the letter. It offers some practical guidance and straight advice for living out the Christian life under Jesus Christ, who has redeemed us and will keep us till that day when we share everlasting glory with Him in heaven. Until then, we have a heap of living to do.

Read **Hebrews 13,** taking note of any verses that encourage you in your faith life. You may want to copy the verses to note cards and place them in places where they will remind you of God's encouragement for you (e.g., **verse 2** by your front door; **verse 4** on your bedside table; **verse 5** in your wallet).

Getting Started

Although this is your last class session, the mutual support of members does not need to end here. Before class, write the name of each class participant on a slip of paper and place the papers in a box. As people arrive, have them choose a name from the box. When all have arrived, read together **verse 18,** then encourage members to pray for one another as they go forth to live what has been learned in this study.

The Class Session

Have a volunteer from the group read aloud "What's Going On Here" from the Study Guide. You may then wish to encourage participants to set aside a time each year to restudy this letter. Then go quickly into the section "Searching the Scriptures."

Searching the Scriptures

Notice that this chapter can be quite easily divided into three sections: social duties **(verses 1–6);** religious duties **(verses 7–17);** and personal instructions **(verses 18–25).** The Study Guide treats the whole section as one, but you may want to make these divisions as you lead the class.

The advice given in this chapter is in the form of an exhortation. God does not intend it as something we "take with a grain of salt." No, these are imperatives for our lives as we witness to the world by living according to the truth of God. We must remember that at all times we live as the forgiven and forgiving children of God.

1. In Christ we are one family, related to one another by His blood and grace, and that crosses all boundaries and barriers.

2. Participants may suggest that we were once strangers to our Lord and that we have been treated with grace and compassion.

3. Jesus said, "Whatever you did for one of the least of these … *you did for Me.*" Jesus accepts our service to God's people as if we were serving Him.

4. God motivates them to make a commitment to each other and empowers them to keep that commitment.

5. Love of money and possessions works against trust in God to supply everything we need. It is also "a root of all kinds of evil" **(1 Timothy 6:10)** in that it fosters evils like thievery, gambling, undersized contributions to church and charity, conflict between management and labor, etc.

6. God will supply everything we need—even in ways we may not expect.

7. God will be with us always and will never forsake us.

8. God is more powerful than any human, and He will, in fact, be there to help in every need.

9. God tells us to remember our leaders—recall with thanksgiving that they spoke the Word of God to us; look at the result—see how they triumphed; imitate their faith—trust as they trusted for God to work through them; obey them—whether we like their decisions or not (as long as we are not ordered to disobey God); submit to them—give them the honor due to God's authoritative servants; make their work "a joy, not a burden."

10. Leaders are accountable to God for us.

11. We are encouraged because it is not our strength and stability we rely on. We know that "He who began [this] good work in [us] will carry it on" **(Philippians 1:6)**.

12. Empty ceremonies and words turn us away from the truth and toward myths and falsehood. God's grace provides the strength to remain true to Christ.

13. We have complete access to Christ, while the Old Testament priests, on the Day of Atonement, could not even eat of the sacrifice **(Leviticus 16:27)**.

14. The writer points us to the eternal city of God, the new Jerusalem, located in heaven. En route we may endure "disgrace."

15. We "sacrifice" through praise—singing praise to the Lord; through confession—speaking of our faith; through good deeds—helping others in various ways; through giving—setting aside a portion of our weekly or monthly income for the Lord.

16. "With such sacrifices God is pleased" **(verse 16).**

17. Something (perhaps his current ministry) prevented the writer from being "restored" soon to the readers. (**Verse 23** suggests that he was not in prison.)

18. Read these verses (printed at the beginning of this session in the Study Guide) together. Invite participants to share in small groups. Through Jesus, God saved us and now motivates and empowers us to do His will. These would be good verses to memorize.

19. Again, discuss in small groups. God encourages us when we hear how He works in a positive manner in the lives of others.

The Word for Us

Note that several questions call for discussion. A few "how" and "why" questions may enhance discussion. *Small-group discussion offers opportunities for more participants to become actively involved. Use that technique as often as time and interest allow.* After discussions, lead participants back into the one theme that dominates not only this chapter but the whole letter—we live by the grace of Jesus! No matter who we are or what we do, no matter our strengths or weaknesses, no matter our faults or failures, we all live only by His grace—now and eternally. If you keep this in mind and emphasize it when questions regarding the faults of others come up, you will help people to know and realize the truth of the last verse of the chapter: "Grace be with you all."

1. We are united in one body in Jesus. Thus there are no boundaries or barriers.

2. God calls us to such a ministry of love, and our Lord Jesus suffered far more rejection than we will.

3. By God's grace and the example of Jesus, we can help one another look beyond the confines of our own lives. Encourage participants to offer practical ways to do this.

4. We can share this word from God through personal witnessing, example, encouragement, forgiveness, etc. Encourage married participants to recommit themselves to their spouse. Remind both married and single members that God asks us all to dedicate ourselves to purity.

5. As is true with any repentant sinner, we can assure that person of God's rich forgiveness in Christ and the promise of the strength of the Holy Spirit to begin anew.

6. Paul felt contentment with what he had in "every situation" because he knew that His Lord would provide for all his needs.

7. Economic security is elusive. We will never be satisfied until we have found our satisfaction in Christ.

8. Accumulation of money and possessions is often motivated by pride. If we are humble, as Christ was **(Matthew 11:29),** we will avoid this error.

9. The Lord is our Helper. Therefore, mere people cannot destroy us or our faith.

10. We owe obedience to government leaders (see **Romans 13:1–7**); support, love, and care to church officials; and support, love, care, encouragement, and a willingness to follow his leading to our pastor. We should pray for all three types of leaders.

11. Encourage volunteers to share opinions.

12. Although we may be convinced we are right and our leaders are wrong, we need to remember that they are God's authorities for our good.

13. As you discuss questions that challenge actions of leaders, remind the group that we all live only and solely by grace.

14. We need to test all teachings against the Word of God to see if they agree with God's teaching. A Christian group proclaims Christ and His grace as the only way to life eternal in heaven.

15. Jesus bore more "disgrace" than we will, and He is keeping us faithful for "an enduring city"—eternal life in heaven.

16. Choose songs that can easily be sung and for which words are readily available.

17. Let your knowledge of your group determine whether you will do this in small groups or with the entire class.

18. Allow time for this speaking and writing; invite sharing in small groups.

Closing

Pray that, as a result of this study, God will have led you and the participants to conclude that

a. we are to live in this world as brothers and sisters in Christ who welcome others and remain committed and contented;

b. as we live by the grace of God alone, we will honor and respect our leaders and pastors and teachers;

c. God gives us the power to give to Him from our wealth, ability, and hearts as we worship, pray, and work together for His glory.

Pray together the prayer written in the Study Guide or have a volunteer lead a prayer. Remind participants that although the structured class sessions are now over, the faith-learning will continue for them every day to come. Thank all class members for their participation and remember to keep them all in your prayers.

Bibliography

Barclay, William. *The Letter to the Hebrews*. Louisville: Westminster/John Knox, 1976.

Bruce, F. F. *Commentary on the Epistle to the Hebrews*. Grand Rapids: William B. Eerdmans Publishing Company, 1990.

Lauersdorf, Richard E. *Hebrews*, The People's Bible Commentary. St. Louis: Concordia Publishing House, 1992.

Lenski, R. C. *The Interpretation of Hebrews and James*. Minneapolis: Augsburg, 1938.

Metzger, Bruce M. *A Textual Commentary on the Greek New Testament*. London: United Bible Societies, 1971, 1975.

Westcott, B. F. *The Epistle to the Hebrews*. London: Macmillan, 1889 (reprinted by Eerdmans).